S0-ALC-614

I would like to dedicate this book to all the laborers in the park; the Lefty McClellans, Woody Hoofards, Jay Muslers, Dennis Haags, and Dave Rudolphs who install the out-houses, paint the buildings, pick up the garbage, maintain the trails, toil to open and maintain the roads, etc. Without men like these there would be no park as we know it. They hardly ever achieve recognition—no retirement parties, few awards, they just fade away.

*George A. Perkins*

Revised edition 1989
Revised edition 1996

A number of facilities at Manzanita Lake have reopened. These are the Loomis Museum, the seismograph station, Reflection Lake picnic area and trail, and the Lily Pond Self-guiding Nature Trail. The Loomis home is scheduled to be opened in 1996 as a year-round ranger station.

The trailhead for the Lily Pond Nature Trail is located directly across the road from the Loomis Museum. It is an easy loop trail one mile in length requiring about one hour's walking time. The trail will take you along lake shores, forest edges and through a portion of the Chaos Jumbles. Attention is drawn to things of interest and beauty which are often overlooked.

The trail around Reflection Lake is an easy, short stroll of 1 mi/1.6 km and takes approximately 30 minutes.

# Introduction

.assen Volcanic National Park was established on August 9, 1916, when Presi-
lent Wilson signed the John Raker Bill, which had just been passed by both
Houses of Congress. Lassen was the 13th National Park. All National Parks are
administered by the U.S. Department of the Interior through the National Park
Service so as to "preserve each park unspoiled for the enjoyment of future as
well as present generations."

The park road is closed in fall after the season's first significant snow-
1. During the winter Lassen Park offers excellent terrain for cross country ski-
g and snow camping. There is no charge to enter the park in the winter and a
e is charged in the summer.

The rangers conduct a full naturalist program during the summer and a
odified one in the winter. Schedules of summer activities are posted at the
ain campgrounds and at park service headquarters in Mineral, California.
hen is the best time to come to visit Lassen Park? The answer, of course, is
enever you can get away. For hikers and backpackers the best time depends
 what provides the most enjoyment. Early summer provides the best photog-
phy and the most mosquitoes. Middle summer provides the best wildflowers
d swimming. A list of normal opening dates is on page 8.

Overnight camping permits are required and may be obtained by writing
rk Superintendent, Lassen Volcanic National Park, Mineral, California 96063
6-595-4444).

Lassen Park has two entrances, the southwest located 9 miles from
neral and the north at Mananzita Lake. Access to them is on Highway 89 and
, and highway 44 and 89 respectively.

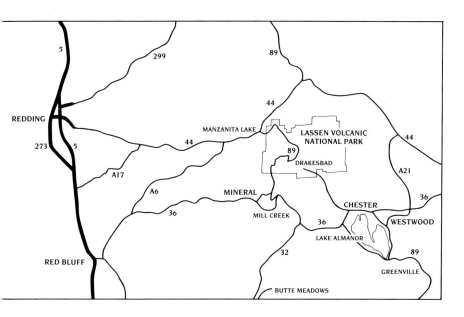

# Preface

Lassen Volcanic National Park is a day hike park. The hikes naturally group themselves according to their trail heads — those from the Park Road, Drakesbad,
Summit, Manzanita, Juniper and Butte Lakes. I've chosen the hikes in that order to
cover the one-hundred and fifty miles of trails in the park. Most of the hikes were
taken in loops and, when possible, from high to low elevations. The reader may
very well wish to change the direction or the combination in order to suit his needs.

Backpacking in the park is accomplished by combining a series of day
hikes. Butte, Summit, Juniper, Horseshoe Lakes and Drakesbad are all within a
day's hike of each other. Summit Lake, because of its accessibility to the park
road, is the most popular 'jumping off' place for backpackers.

I didn't go into a great deal of detail concerning the botany, geology, birds,
and zoology as these subjects are well covered by other books listed on page 99.

I have attempted to give the average hiker an explanation along with
color pictures of what he might expect to see when he gets there, as well as
what he might see along the way.

I want to express my appreciation to Richard L. Vance, the former Chief
Park Naturalist of Lassen Volcanic National Park, without whose help this book
would not be possible. I would like to give acknowledgment to Paul E. Schultz
for providing the history portion from his book, *Lassen's Place Names*. And I would
like to extend my thanks to Betty Knight, former Chief Park Naturalist of Lassen,
for her assistance in editing this third and most extensive revision of the book.

# For the Novice Hiker

Items to take day hiking:
> Full Canteen
> Map
> Watch (optional — see notes)
> Optional: Compass, Band-Aids, trail mix, fruit, camera with extra
> film, chewing gum, light jacket or sweater, extra pair of socks, sun
> tan lotion, mosquito repellant, and sun glasses.

1. **Stay on the established trail**   Don't shortcut. Shortcutting not only increases the
chances of becoming lost, but adds to the erosion of the soils.

2. **Plan your hike**   Allow enough time to enjoy your hike; allocate plenty of time
before darkness. Time your average pace so you can estimate how long the
hike will take. Most hikers travel at 1½ to 2 miles an hour. If you have gone well
past your time, you may have taken the wrong fork or gone by your destination.

3. **If the trail becomes obliterated** due to a falling snag or some other reason, first
look ahead for the red or yellow trail markers nailed to trees. Also look for
downed trees that have been sawed into. If none are visible, retrace your steps
until you come to a trail marker.

4. **Children** tire more easily than adults so it is best to take them on shorter hikes. It is also better to take them on hikes which climb initially so that the return is downhill.

5. **Don't litter!** A candy or gum wrapper, a film box, or a cigarette butt may seem like a small item to throw away, but in the forest it mars the beauty. People who throw away trash are just what the name implies — trash.

6. **Wear Proper Clothing**   Light hiking boots are best. Tennis shoes are o.k. for hikes that are short and mostly level. Remember that in early summer trails may be free of snow at the trailhead, but as the trails gain in elevation, snow will most likely be traversed. Clothing should be loose and light with a sweater or light jacket worn around the waist for hikes that gain in elevation.

7. **Careful with fire.**   Know the regulations—No wood fires in back country. Use back packing fuel stoves. They are more efficient and much safer. Do not smoke while hiking.

8. **Know the regulations**   For example: overnight camping permits are required. No animals (except horses) are allowed on the trails. Horses are not permitted on some sections of trails. Camping is not allowed within one-quarter mile of fifty areas. Regulations, particularly those concerning fire, change from year to year, so check with the Park Service.

# Common Questions

*Why doesn't the park service clean up the forest cuttings and dead snags by removing or con-trol-burning to eliminate the forest debris, and harvest the dying mature trees for lumber?*

The forest service which controls the vast majority of timber lands utilizes the forest as a crop, applying forest management techniques. However the philosophy of the National Park Service is to leave things in as natural and untouched a state as possible. Although this might not always be esthetically beautiful in our eyes, it does provide the ecological balance as nature evolved. An example would be nature providing insects, which harbor in dead trees, which in turn the birds feed on for their survival. Another consideration is in the tree life cycle, which consists of hundreds of years. How can we really tell at this point, by leaving things in a natural state, wouldn't we in the long run provide a more beautiful forest?

*Why are those rocks or limbs laid across the trail?*

They are not there to keep you awake or test the agility of your horse. They are called water breaks. They prevent erosion of the trail by diverting run-off water and keeping it off the trail.

*Where is the best area in the park to observe birds?*

Though a great variety of birds inhabit the entire park, the Manzanita Lake area is considered the best place in the park to observe our feathered friends.

Is *the water in the streams and lakes in the park safe to drink?*
Due to the outbreak of giardia in the Sierra Nevada, water must be treated or filtered.

Why *are the lodging and dining facilities no longer in operation at Manzanita Lake?*
Up until 1974 the park concession operated a complete mountain resort at Manzanita Lake, However, in 1974 Dwight R. Crandell published "Chaos Crags Eruptions and Rock Fall Avalanches in Lassen Volcanic Park, California" in the U.S. Geological Survey Journal of Research. This paper stated that there was a serious hazard of a rock fall avalanche recurring similar to the one which happened approximately 200 years before. The concession's facilities were within the hazard area. The concessionaire requested the Park Service to guarantee the safety of its employees and guests. This was not possible and the Park Service chose at this point to purchase the concessionaire's interest and to close the facilities.

# Park Regulations

1. STAY ON ESTABLISHED TRAILS AT ALL TIMES, ESPECIALLY IN THERMAL AREAS. KEEP CHILDREN UNDER CONTROL, GROUND CRUSTS ARE OFTEN DANGEROUSLY THIN.

2. Camping is limited to 14 days year-round except at Lost Creek and Summit Lake. Limitation at these areas is 7 days. When the limit has been reached, you may not move to another campground in the park for another period of stay,

3. Camping fees of $10.00 per day are charged at Manzanita Lake and North Summit Lake. A fee of $8.00 is charged at Warner Valley. At South Summit Lake and Southwest Campgrounds, a $6.00 fee is charged. Golden Age Passport holders are entitled to a 50% discount on campground fees. Butte Lake Campground is closed for camping but open for day use. All campground and group campground fees and use are subject to change. Please refer to the Lassen Park Guide distributed at entrance stations for current information.

4. Campsites are not to be disturbed by cutting plants or digging the ground.

5. Camp only in designated sites. Do not drive beyond the barrier logs or rocks designating the sites. Do not camp along the roads or in parking lots. No motor vehicles or bicycles are allowed on trails. Skateboards are not allowed on park roads, including campground roads, or on trails. A wilderness permit is required when camping anywhere other than in a designated campground. Wilderness permits are available at some Park Service Ranger Stations, Park Headquarters, Loomis Museum, and Almanor and Hat Creek Forest Service Ranger Stations.

6. Leave a camp as clean as you found it or cleaner.

7. No camp in the park may be used as a base for hunting outside the park.

8. Visitors shall not wash clothing, cooking, eating utensils in or, pollute in any other manner, such as cleaning fish, any waters in the park.

Hiking Trails of Lasse

9. Please observe quiet hours from 10 P.M. to 8 A.M.

10. Fireplaces are in most developed campgrounds and must be used where provided. No open fires. **NEVER LEAVE A FIRE UNATTENDED.**

11. **FIREWOOD:** Wood from dead and down trees may be used. Use of wood from standing trees, live or dead, is prohibited. Wood gathering is not permitted in the Devastated Area. Firewood is scarce in the park and the use of portable stoves is encouraged. Use of chain saws is prohibited.

12. The use of fireworks, firecrackers, or firearms in the park is prohibited.

13. *Dogs and cats* are permitted in the park, but must be kept on a leash, crated, or otherwise under physical restrictive control at all times. Pets are not permitted on trails, swimming beaches, at evening programs or in public buildings.

14. The feeding, touching, teasing or molesting of native birds or mammals is prohibited. Feeding of wildlife can make them dependent on man and therefore cause them to die when they must forage for themselves. Animals sometimes carry diseases which can be transmitted to man. Bears occasionally visit campgrounds. Precautions should be taken to store food items.

15. *Privately owned boats* are permitted on all park lakes except Emerald Lake, Lake Helen, Reflection Lake and Boiling Springs Lake. Power motors, including electric, are not permitted on any park waters. A personal flotation device is required for each occupant in the boat. No boat rentals are available.

16. *Fishing* in the park is in accordance with California and local fishing regulations. A California fishing license is required. No bait collecting in the park.

17. Never swim alone; know the area in which you are swimming.

18. No electric, water or sewer connections for trailers are available in park.

19. All campground facilities are available on a first come, first served basis. No reservations can be made.

20. *The fee system* for Lassen Volcanic National Park is established by Congress. A $5.00 single visit vehicle permit shall admit the purchaser and all other passengers in private noncommercial vehicle for entrance. Buses and organized groups have a different fee structure. Yearly and Golden Age permits are also available. Fees are subject to change.

21. Kings Creek and Emerald Picnic Areas, and picnic areas at Summit Lake, Butte Lake and Warner Valley campgrounds, are available for day use only.

22. Opening and closing dates are dependent on weather and snow conditions.

23. *Wilderness permits* are required for all overnight stays in the backcountry. Permits will not be issued for camping within one mile of developed areas, camp-

grounds or park roads and areas identified as closed to overnight camping. Permits are issued on a one trip basis. A new permit must be obtained for each trip. Permits are available on arrival at Park Headquarters or at all ranger stations and there is no fee. They can also be requested by telephone or mail, two weeks in advance. Requests should be directed to: **Superintendent, Lassen Volcanic National Park, Mineral, California 96063   (916) 595-4444.**

A wilderness permit for joint use of the Lassen Park and Caribou wilderness areas can be obtained from the agency in which the trip originates.

24. *Pack and saddle stock* may not overnight anywhere in the park, except in the cor rals at Summit Lake and Juniper Lake. Advance reservations are recommended. No grazing is allowed. All feed must be brought into the park and residual feed removed when leaving.

Stock groups are limited to 15 animals. A wilderness permit is required for all day use of stock in the park. A small corral is available near the northern park boundary for Pacific Crest Trail users.

25.  Make your toilet away from campsites and at least 100 feet from the nearest water supply or trail. Bury it.

26.  Don't construct improvements, such as rock walls, large fireplaces, bough beds, tables, rock and log stream crossings, etc.

# Lassen Campgrounds

| | | | |
|---|---|---|---|
| Butte Lake | Day use only No overnight camping | June 6- Oct. 15 | Fishing, Swimming, Hiking to nearby Cinder Cone and Snag Lake. Boating without motors. Fireplaces, tables, no piped water, chemical toilet, garbage collection. |
| Warner Valley | 15 sites | June 13 - Oct. 1 | Stream fishing, hiking. Fireplaces, tables, piped water, pit toilets, garbage collection. Nearest supplies in Chester. Not recommended for trailers. Meals (on reservation), cold drinks, telephone and horseback riding available at Drakesbad Guest Ranch. |
| Juniper Lake | 18 sites | Late June - Oct. 1 | Fishing, Swimming in lake. Boating without motors. Fireplaces, tables, pit toilets. Water from lake should be boiled. |
| Manzanita Lake | 179 sites | June - Oct. 15 | Fireplaces, tables, flush toilets, piped water, garbage collection, trailer dumping station. Will accommodate 35' trailers. |
| Crags | 45 sites | June - Oct. | Fireplaces, tables, piped water, chemical toilets, |

8

|  |  |  | garbage collection. Will accommodate 35′ trailers. |
|---|---|---|---|
| Southwest | 21 sites | June 13-Oct. 1 | Walk-in campsites, fireplaces, tables, piped water, comfort station w/flush toilets, garbage collection. Lassen Chalet (open business hrs. in summer) has food service and gift shop. |
| Summit Lake | 94 sites | June-Sept. 15 | Fireplaces, tables, flush toilets (north campground), garbage collection. |

The areas below are closed to camping for 1/4 mile in all directions.

Boiling Springs Lake
Bumpass Hell & Trail
Butte Lake (except south end)
Cinder Cone
Cliff Lake
Cold Boiling Lake
Cold Spring
Crags Lake
Crumbaugh Lake
Crystal Lake
Devil's Kitchen
Dream Lake
Echo Lake
Hat Creek: East Fork
Hat Creek: West Fork
  (between park road
  and main stream)
Hat Creek Cabin Area
Hat Lake
Hot Springs Creek
  (Devil's Kitchen to
  South Boundary)
Inspiration Point
Juniper Lake
  (except campground)
Kings Creek Falls
Lassen Peak
  (Summit & Trail)
Little Hot Springs Valley
Manzanita Creek (below
  bridge to Sec. 29)
Manzanita Lake
Mt. Harkness (Summit)
Shadow Lake
Soda Lake
Terrace Lake
Warner Valley

# Resorts and Facilities

**Mineral Lodge** — Located 42 miles east of Red Bluff on State Highway 36, 9 miles from the southwest entrance station. This lodge offers motel rooms, housekeeping cabins, a general store, restaurant and bar, gift shop and swimming pool. Write Mineral Lodge, Mineral, CA 96063; 916-595-4422.

**Mineral Gas Mart** — Offers gasoline, deli, and mini mart. P.O. Box 10, Mineral, CA 96063; 916-595-3222.

**Volcano Country RV Park** — Offers laundromat, post office, health food store, propane and dump station. Write P.O. Box 55, Mineral, CA 96063; 916-595-3347.

**Mill Creek Resort** — Located 6 miles from Mineral on Highway 172. It offers a general store, cafe, housekeeping cabins, trailer spaces and post office. Write Mill Creek Resort, Mill Creek, CA 96061; 916-595-4449.

**Childs Meadows** — Closed at time of publication.

**Fire Mountain Lodge** — Located 57 miles east of Red Bluff on Highway 36, 15 miles from the southwest entrance station. It offers a small general store, cabins, restaurant and bar and a trailer park. Write Fire Mountain Lodge, Rt. 5, Box 3500, Mill Creek, CA 96061; 916-258-2938.

**Deer Creek Lodge** — Located east of the Highway 32 junction west of Black Forest Lodge. Has housekeeping cabins, restaurant and bar. Write Deer Creek Lodge, Rt. 5, Box 4000, Mill Creek, CA 96061; 916-258-2939.

**Black Forest Lodge** — This lodge can be found 3 miles east of the Highway 32 junction on Highway 36. It offers rooms, a bar, and specializes in good German food. Write Black Forest Lodge, Rt. 5, Box 5000, Mill Creek, CA 96061; 916-258-2941.

**St. Bernard Lodge** — Located .1 of a mile east of Black Forest Lodge on Highway 36. It offers a restaurant and bar and rooms. Write St. Bernard Lodge, Box 493, Chester, CA 96020;916-258-3382.

**Chester California** — This is a small town which has a population of 3300. It has several markets, banks, motels, etc. and serves as a jumping off place for Drakesbad 17 miles, Warner Valley Campground 16 miles, and Juniper Lake Campground 11.7 miles.

**Drakesbad Guest Ranch** — Operated by the Park Service Concession, it is the only resort operating inside the park. It offers cabins, telephone, thermal pool, meals and horseback riding. Write 2150 Main #7, Red Bluff, CA 96080; 916-529-1512.

**Hat Creek Resort** — Located on State Highway 89, 3 miles southwest of the Highway 44 junction near Old Station, 10.4 miles northeast of Highway 44 junction near Lassen Park. It offers a small store, cabins, restaurant, post office and gasoline. Write Box 15, Old Station, CA 96071; 916-335-7121.

Hiking Trails of Lassen

# 1 Brokeoff Mountain

*From Park Road*

**TRAILHEAD:** Road guide marker #2, .5 of a mile from Southern boundary of Lassen Volcanic National Park

**FEATURES:** Lakes, meadows, wildflowers, forest and majestic views

**DISTANCE:** 3.5 miles (5.7 km) to the summit and return for total of 7.0 miles (11.3 km). Additional .3 of a mile (.5 km) to Forest Lake and return.

**TIME:** Allow 4 hours

**WILDLIFE:** Deer, Grouse, Eagle

**HISTORY:** The name Brokeoff is derived from the topography of the mountain which resulted from the movement along a great fault which caused the major (north) part of the large ancestral volcano, Mt. Tehama, to sink far below the more stable Brokeoff rim remnant which we see today.

**AUTHOR'S COMMENTS:** This hike combines almost all the features one would expect in a good mountain hike. It climbs a peak with views in every direction. The trail crosses and follows springs running through meadows with wildflowers and passes unusual rock formations.

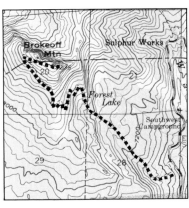

The trail starts next to a stream which initiates near Forest Lake, and flows into Mill Creek. The trail proceeds to the south, in the opposite direction of Brokeoff Mountain. It climbs moderately through Alders, a section that can be wet and muddy in the spring. In less than .1 of a mile, it swings west through a forest of Western Pine and Red Fir, with a ground cover of grass and Pinemat Manzanita. After approximately .3 of a mile from the start, the trail turns northwest with Brokeoff in prominent view to the forefront. It passes a small lakelet on the left, and follows the stream which provides the moisture for the meadows and wildflowers, including Blue and White Stick Seed, Mountain Heather, and Senecio. There are talus slopes (rock slides) above to the left, and after another .2 of a mile, there are interesting lava boulders.

Approximately 1.3 miles from the start, the main trail swings left, leaves the meadow area, and starts a steep ascent. (There is an unmarked trail which continues to parallel the meadows to the right, going to Forest Lake approximately .1 of a mile further.) The main trail provides a view of Forest Lake and it's suggested that the decision to go to Forest Lake be delayed as it can be visited on the return. The trail continues its steep to moderate ascent all the way to the summit. Mountain Hemlock, Heather and Silver Leaf Lupine appear as the trail increases in elevation. Approximately .2 of a mile from the viewpoint of Forest Lake, Mount Conard and Lake Almanor are in view to the East. After 2.0 miles from the start, the trail turns west for .1 of a mile, and then switches back and forth with a view of Child's Meadow to the southeast. Most of the forest of Mountain Hemlock has evidence of snow bend and damage. As the trail continues to climb, there are more interesting rock formations, and Mt. Harkness is visible to the east. After approximately 2.5 miles from the start, there is a Mountain Hemlock with 8 trees growing from the same base. It is where the trail makes its last switchback to the southwest below the base of Brokeoff. Afternoon thunder showers are common in the summer, and if they are threatening, it is best not to proceed up the ridge top to the summit because of the lightning danger.

Approximately 2.7 miles from the start, the trail goes north along the west side of Brokeoff. Mineral Meadows and the Sacramento Valley are in view to the left. It proceeds for .6 of a mile, and switches back for its final ascent. The trail at this point is near timber line in the alpine zone. Prominent ground cover is Pennyroyal, and wildflowers include Indian and Lassen Paint Brush, Royal Penstemon and Sulphur Flowers. The summit has views of Lassen Peak and Lake   to the northeast and Mt. Diller and the edge of old Mt. Tehama to the north. Brokeoff Meadows seems like a miniature golf course. To the south, Heart and Huckleberry Lakes and Mineral and Glass Burner Meadows are in view. To the west is the Sacramento Valley and the Coast Range. To the south is the Sierra Nevada which starts just south of Mineral and Child's Meadows.

# 2 Ridge Lakes
*From Park Road*

**TRAILHEAD:** Sulphur Works Parking Lot

**FEATURES:** Lakes, flowers, scenic views, wildlife, forests

**DISTANCE:** 1.0 miles (1.6 km) one way

**TIME:** 1½ hours hiking. Allow extra time for swimming or resting at Ridge Lakes.

8000'
7600'
7200'
6800'

AVERAGE GRADE 20%

MILES .5  1.0

Hiking Trails of Lassen

dge Lakes trail is comparatively steep with a steady rise in elevation. It has an

undance of wildflow-
s and there is a good
ossibility of spotting
eer. It has beautiful
ews of Brokeoff and
t. Diller, part of the
est rim of old Mt.
hama. A few minutes
own the trail is a view
the Sulphur Works
d towards the south-
ast, a view of Childs
eadows. About 15 min-
es from the start, there
an excellent place to
ink and refill your can-
en with the cold water
om West Sulphur
eek. The steady ascent
the trail provides one
th just enough exer-
on to make swimming
Ridge Lake that much
ore exhilarating. When
e lakes are full, they
in. Wildflowers include
eopard Lily, Lupine,
oyote Mint, California
tterweed.

# 3 Sulphur Works
*Park Road*

**RAILHEAD:** Guide post #5, just North of the parking lot on
Lassen Park Road

**FEATURES:** Hydrothermal activity

**DISTANCE:** .2 of a mile (.3 km) round trip

**TIME:** 20 minutes

**HISTORY:** The site derived its name from a commercial

operation started in 1865 to mine sulphur. The operation was under the direction of Dr. Supan, and was called "Supan's Sulphur Works." The Supan heirs conducted a private tourist facility until the site was obtained in the early fifties by the federal government.

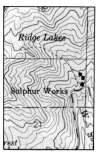

**AUTHOR'S COMMENTS:** This short hike right off the Park road is a must for those travelling through Lassen. If you enjoy it, and want to see more, you can consider taking the short hike into Bumpass Hell for a similar but much larger area.

This short hike is the only one in the Park that can be taken in a wheelchair. There are handicap reserved parking spaces in the lot with suitable ramps. This active area of bubbling mud pots, fumaroles, with hydrogen sulphide gas has signs explaining the area along the way. The Sulphur Works is considered to be remnants of the main vent of Mt. Tehama. Mt. Tehama is estimated to have been 11,000 feet high, and eventually collapsed. The rock is decomposing under the constant action of sulphuric acids. The area is more active in the winter, and it is a short cross-country ski trip along the snow-covered Park road from the Ski Area. Visitors are warned to stay on the established trails.

# 4 Mill Creek Falls
*From Park Road and return*

**TRAILHEAD:** North end of the Southwest Walk-in Campground.

**FEATURES:** Wildflowers, forest, waterfall and views

**DISTANCE:** 1.6 miles (2.6 km) to Mill Creek Falls, Overlook — Mill Creek Falls 1.7 miles (2.8 km), Conard Meadows 2.5 miles (4.0 km), Crumbaugh Lake 3.4 miles (5.5 km), Cold Boiling Lake 4.4 miles (7.1 km), Kings Creek 5.1 miles (8.2 km)

**TOPOGRAPHY:** Slightly undulating

**TIME:** Allow 2 to 2½ hours

**WILDLIFE:** Mountain Quail, Deer

6800'
6400'
6000'
MILL CREEK FALLS
MILES .5  1.0  1.5  2.0

**HISTORY:** Mill Creek Falls is formed just below the confluence of East Sulphur Creek and Bumpass Hell Creek, forming the headwaters of Mill Creek. Mill Creek was named in 1843 by John Bidwell when he, Peter Lassen, Burnheim, and an Indian guide came upon the stream in the Sacramento Valley. Bidwell states, "The next flowing stream having still more fall where we crossed it suggested its value as a fine water power, so we named it Mill Creek."

**AUTHOR'S COMMENTS:** This trail is a relatively easy hike, and suitable for children and older persons, as all rises are followed by levels or descents that provide natural rest. Another way to view the Falls is to start from the trailhead at the Kings Creek Picnic Area — road marker #30, and return (page 24), or make arrangements for transportation and hike from Kings Creek to the Sulphur Works Campground 5.1 miles one way.

he trail descends for .2 of a mile where it crosses West Sulphur Creek. The Red ir forest is not inspiring in this section, but it affords a contrast to the lovely rest which follows. After crossing the creek, the trail ascends an open hillside f wildflowers. For approximately .1 of a mile, the trail proceeds in an easterly di- ction, and after approximately .5 of a mile, you can hear running water from an nnamed creek fork. The forest in this section is beautiful Red Fir (Silvertip) with any of the younger trees being perfect examples of the classic Christmas tree. hough not in abundance in this section of the trail, there are many varieties of ildflowers.

After approximately 1.0 miles, the trail crosses a small mountain rivulet here you can replenish your water supply or have a drink. The trail is well arked with the familiary yellow discs and is easy to follow. Approximately .3 of mile further from the small rivulet, there are some interesting lava rock forma- ons. A short distance past the lava rock, Mt. Conard comes into view on the ght or towards the south. You can hear the falls approximately .1 of a mile be- re arriving to view them. The viewing spot is just off the trail to the right, and are should be taken, as the drop off the trail is quite steep. The falls are approx- ately 75 feet high — the longest in the Park. It is formed by the junction of ast Sulphur and Bumpass Hell Creeks. The trail continues on to Conard Mead- ws .9 of a mile, Crumbaugh Lake 1.8 miles, Cold Boiling Lake 2.8 miles, and ings Creek Picnic Area 3,5 miles further. The return trip provides majestic views f Brokeoff, Mt. Diller, and Pilot Pinnacle to the forefront (west).

# 5 Bumpass Hell
*Park Road to Bumpass Hell, Cold Boiling Lake and the Kings Creek Picnic Area*

**RAILHEAD:** Road guide markers #16 and #17, Bumpass Hell Parking Lot

**FEATURES:** Forest, lakes, scenic views, wildlife, hydrothermal activity

**DISTANCE:** Bumpass Hell 1.5 miles (2.4 km), Cold Boiling Lake 3.4 miles (5.5 km), Kings Creek picnic area 4.0 miles (6.5 km)

**TIME:** Allow 2½ hours one way

**HISTORY:** Bumpass Hell was named after Kendall V. Bumpass who discovered it in 1864. History has it that in 1865, while guiding the editor of the Red Bluff Independent Newspaper, he broke through the crust and plunged his leg into the boiling mud beneath, burning him severely. His comment was that "the descent to Hell was easy."

**AUTHOR'S COMMENTS:** Most hikers go to Bumpass Hell and return to the parking lot. However, if you are a group, a suggestion is to have one of your group pick you up at the Kings Creek picnic area. By the time they returned to the Bumpass Hell parking lot and drove to the picnic area at Kings Creek, there would be very little wait for either party.

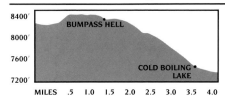

This hike is probably Lassen Park's most popular. Bumpass Hell consists of 16 acres of hydrothermal activity — the largest in the Park. The trail is self-guiding and reprinted on page 75. The forest is White Bark Pine and Mountain Hemlock. There are distinct views to the west of the Mount Tehama Cauldron with Mt. Conard, Brokeoff Mountain, Mt. Diller, and Pilot Pinnacle. Ground cover is Silverleaf Lupine, Pinemat Manzanita, Mountain Heather, and Bog Kalmia.

The trail ascends 250 feet and then descends 200 feet into Bumpass Hell. Bumpass Hell consists of 3 or 4 main vents and many minor ones spewing forth steam. There are many mud pots and fumaroles. For safety reasons, the Park Service has built a system of wooden tressels to walk on which lead to all the main vents. It's imperative that you stay on the wooden walks, as crust forms over mud pots and you can break through into boiling water and mud.

The vast majority of hikers return to the parking lot, however, the trail continues to Cold Boiling Lake and Kings Creek picnic area. The trail junction is marked just as you enter the floor of Bumpass Hell on the right: Cold Boiling Lake 1.9 miles (3.0 km), Crumbaugh Lake 2.4 miles (3.8 km), Kings Creek picnic area 2.5 miles (4.0 km). The trail proceeds along the south edge of Bumpass Hell, then ascends out of the bowl for .2 of a mile, levels for .1 of a mile and then starts a descent to Cold Boiling Lake. After .5 of a mile from Bumpass Hell, there are scenic views of Mt. Conard and the Mineral Meadows to the forefront. The headwaters of East Sulphur Creek can be seen and heard in the Valley below. Five tenths of a mile further, there is a good view of Crumbaugh Lake.

ter another .2 of a mile, Cold Boiling Lake and Reading Peak are in view. The
ail descends rapidly to Cold Boiling Lake. From Cold Boiling Lake to Kings
eek is described in reverse on page 15, hike from "Kings Creek to Southwest
ampground Via Cold Boiling Lake, Crumbaugh Lake and Mill Creek Falls." Two
nths of a mile (.3 km) past Cold Boiling Lake, the trail to Twin Meadows
rks to the right 1.9 miles (3.0 km), Kings Creek after .5 of a mile (.8 km) of
vel trail arrives at Kings Creek picnic area.

# 6 Lassen Peak
*Park Road to summit*

**TRAILHEAD:** Parking lot at the summit of the Park road sign marker # 22

**FEATURES:** Vistas of volcanoes, lakes, forests, thermal activity

**DISTANCE:** 2.5 miles (4.0 km) one way

**TIME:** Allow 3 to 4 hours

**HISTORY:** *Lassen Peak* is named after Peter Lassen, a Danish blacksmith who emigrated to Northern California. He obtained a Mexican land grant near the present site of Vina. Here he founded a town called Benton City. He guided immigrants over his own Lassen Trail in order to insure that they would arrive at Benton City to buy necessary items to re-supply. He moved to the Honey Lake region and was killed by parties unknown near Black Rock, Nevada in November 1859. Lassen Peak has had many names, both by Indians and white men. Among them are Sister Buttes, San Jose, Mount Saint Joseph, Lassen's Butte, Lawson's Butte, Snow Mountain, Snow Butte, and in recent times, Mt. Lassen.

e trail proceeds up a rather steep incline with a forest of scattered Mountain
emlock. The ground cover is sparse. After .5 of a mile, Lake Almanor is in view
the southeast, and the meadows of the town of Mineral to the southwest.
ter approximately .8 of a mile, the Mountain Hemlock gives way to gnarled
nite Bark Pine. Brokeoff and Diller are the prominent peaks to the west, Mt.
nard to the south, and Reading Peak to the east. After 1.0 miles, the Sacramento
lley is visible to the west and Shadow Lake to the east. The trail mileage signs
e distances remaining to the top, not distances travelled. The trail zig-zags its
y to the summit, where an entire view of the Park awaits you, as well as Mt.
asta, which is visible to the north. On occasion, there are whiffs of steam from
e crater as a reminder of Lassen Peak's classification as an active volcano.

*The Lassen Peak trail leaflet text is reprinted as follows:*

Zig-zagging 2.2 miles to the top of one of the world's largest plug domes,
e Lassen Peak Trail offers magnificent vistas of a land of volcanoes, mountain

forests and sparkling lakes. Four types of volcanoes can be seen from the trail. The summit of the peak is crowned by several craters and the lava flow of 1915.

A round trip takes about four hours for the average person. A slow pace is advised at this elevation (8,500 to 10,457). For your comfort, take *suntan lotion*, dark glasses, a hat, water and *a wind breaker*. Be prepared for strong winds at the summit, even though it may be calm when you start your trip. *PLEASE* stay on the trail.

Lassen Peak lies at the southern tip of the Cascade Range, a series of volcanic mountains that extend through Northern California, Oregon, Washington and on into Canada. Lassen and the Cascade Range are in turn a part of the Circle of Fire, a series of volcanoes that ring the Pacific Ocean. They owe their existence to the drifting of the continents upon the earth's crust. Thus, Asia and America are moving closer together and overriding the floor of the Pacific Ocean

Tremendous forces are at work, faults occur and molten material, perhaps from the ocean floor that has dipped below the Pacific Coast, can return to the earth's surface as lava.

Today the Lassen region is a land of earthquakes and volcanoes, but it has not always been so. Seventy million years ago, a seaway, "the Lassen Strait," flowed through this area connecting the Pacific Ocean with an inland sea in Eastern Oregon. So the Lassen region has a long history of change; change that still continues.

About 27,000 years ago, while glaciers still mantled this region, a one-cubic mile dome of semi-solid lava thrust from the earth. Lassen's creation would have been a terrifying event to witness. Enormous earthquakes must have reverberated across this land as this massive volcano shoved aside the overlying rock. The peak reached its full height in perhaps five years — a short time for such a huge dome — then it plugged its vent by virtue of its own size and weight, hence the name plug dome volcano.

Much of the dome is hidden by the talus which formed as the lava cooled and fractured, but outcroppings reveal the steepness of the original dome. Glaciers have left signatures in the form of small moraines on the talus slopes.

Except for the occasional minor eruptions every few hundred years, the peak was quiet after its rise. The Indians, Spanish and American pioneers knew Lassen Peak as a peaceful quiet mountain.

Suddenly, on May 30, 1914, the peak erupted once more. Over 150 steam explosions continued through the following year, piling volcanic debris and ash on the deep snow pack on the volcano's slopes. Then on May 19, 1915, lava welled up in the throat of the volcano and spilled over notches in the summit. The glowing mass flowed 1,000 feet down the western slope and cooled. But on the steeper eastern flank, the lava broke off in chunks and combined with snow and ash to form a massive mudflow that swept down the mountain and beyond for 18 miles. A quarter-mile wide swath was cut through the forest.

Three days later a violent eruption shook the peak and blasted volcanic debris five miles into the air. Ash was dumped as far as Reno, though a portion of the *Great Hot Blast* was deflected down over the path of the mudflow, widening it by snapping trees like matches for a distance of three miles. Today this Devastated Area is in the process of healing, but it is still a reminder of the mountain's power.

Minor eruptions continued until 1921, and steam was visible in summit

aters until the early 1940's. Only thin wisps of steam are visible upon close spection today.

Will the peak erupt again? No one knows. It seems unlikely, but as long the continents continue to drift, volcanic activity is apt to continue in the cific Circle of Fire. So the peak and surrounding volcanoes are being closely onitored via satellite, infrared photography from aircraft and seismographs.

Plant survival on the rocky slopes of Lassen Peak is difficult and growth is w in the harsh environment. Driving winds suppress size; long winters, twenty-ot snowpacks and bitter temperatures shorten the growing season; lack of soil duces fertility; and high elevations increase exposure to, and allow penetration oppressive solar radiation.

Still, plants adapt. Many have small and waxy leaves to conserve moisture, d extra pigment to resist radiation. Others have extensive root systems to sure nourishment. All have rapid growth in warm weather of a short season.

With these characteristics, a few flowers are able to survive at the summit. arled White Bark Pine creep higher up Lassen slopes than any other tree but l to reach the summit. At lower elevations, Mountain Hemlock and Western nite Pine dominate.

Mammals are not too common, but occasionally a ground squirrel or cket gopher reaches the summit. Hawks and eagles often nest on inaccessible gs. A myriad of insects — including damselflies, dragonflies, bees, and butter-es — abound at the summit, carried there by the updrafts of wind.

Most characteristic of these barren rocky slopes is the pika, a small, grayish, unded-eared relative of the rabbit. You may see one. If you are not fortunate ough to see these elusive animals, you may hear their harsh, high-pitched call ere the trail crosses the talus slopes.

With time, soil will develop and other forms of life will dot the slopes of ssen Peak. But above treeline, weather and the silent mountain will always minate.

# 7 Terrace, Shadow, Cliff & Summit Lakes

**TRAILHEAD:** Guide Marker #27 on Park Road

**FEATURES:** Lakes, swimming, forest, wildflowers

**DISTANCE:** Terrace Lake .5 of a mile (.8 km), Shadow Lake .8 of a mile (1.2 km), Cliff Lake 1.7 miles (2.7 km), Paradise Meadow 1.6 miles (2.6 km), Hat Lake 2.8 miles (4.6 km), Summit Lake Ranger Station 3.9 miles (6.3 km)

**TIME:** 2½ hours one way

**HISTORY:** *Terrace Lake* is the smallest of the three so-called White lakes. Named because the lake is situated on a natural step or terrace above Shadow Lake.

*Shadow Lake*: This 1,100 foot lake is situated in a small deep glacier basin, cirque-like in form, open to the east. Being close to the walls, the lake is in shadows most of the time.

*Cliff Lake*: So named because it lies at the north base of the abrupt cliff-like face of Reading Peak (a plug dome volcano).

*Summit Lake*: originally called Duck Lake. Its name stems from its location atop a slightly convex plateau. Drainage from this area runs both north into the Pit River and south into the Feather River.

**AUTHOR'S COMMENTS:** This is a good hike for children and adults who aren't in good shape, as it is almost all downhill. The best way is to leave your car at Summit Lake and make arrangements for transportation to road guide marker #27. It's also a good short hike for swimming. Just park at road marker #27 and hike the .5 of a mile to Terrace Lake, and return. (Remember the water doesn't warm on Terrace till late July or August.) If you are going as far as Cliff Lake and return, it is uphill all the way back, so

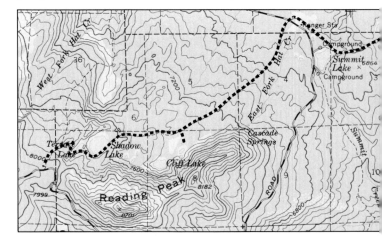

judge the difficulty of the return when considering how far you are going. This is one of the last trails in the Park to be free of snow.

The trail descends moderately for .2 of a mile, then forks with the left going to Paradise Meadow 1.4 miles and Hat Lake 2.7 miles, and the right going .3 of a mile downhill to Terrace Lake. The forest is almost entirely Mountain Hemlock. This small beautiful mountain lake is ideal for swimming, especially from the south end where the trail enters the edge. It has a sand and gravel bottom with a grassy beach. Because of its elevation (7,800), the best time for swimming is late July and August. The forest around the lake is fairly open with mostly Western White Pine and Mountain Hemlock. The trail rises and descends .3 of a mile into Shadow Lake. A good spot for swimming in this lake is also where the trail enters the edge. Lupine is common along the trail. The trail continues around the south and east sides of Shadow Lake (elev. 7,600) with a gradual descent for approximately .5 of a mile when the trail to Cliff Lake branches off to the right. It is well marked by a Park Service sign. During the descent, the forest changes from Mountain Hemlock to Red Fir, and Reading Peak is visible to the right (south). The trail to Cliff Lake winds .2 of a mile through a dense forest of Red Fir, Lodgepole and Western White Pine. Lupine and Heather are evident. Where the trail enters the lake on its north side is the outlet stream, and the area is profuse with wildflowers. The south side of the lake has white cliffs and rock slides, hence the name. In the center is a small island, and the lake has a green tinge similar to Emerald Lake.

Rejoining the main trail, it proceeds for a level .5 of a mile, where it crosses and parallels a small brook that comes out of Cliff Lake. This area is also abundant in wildflowers. Clark's nutcracker is one of the birds that inhabit this area. The trail levels and then comes out on a ridge of Manzanita and Fir, and then has a series of gradual to moderate descents, with an open view of Hat Mountain to the forefront. This area appears to have had a fire many years ago. After .2 of a mile through the Manzanita, the trail descends through heavy timber, ending at the Park road, marker #38. It is .5 of a mile south to Summit Lake.

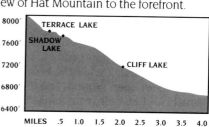

# 8 Soda Lake

**TRAILHEAD:** Lassen Peak Parking Area, guide marker #22

**FEATURES:** Lake, wildflowers

**DISTANCE:** Approximately 2.0 miles (3.2 km) one way

**TOPOGRAPHY:** Rises for approximately 300 feet, then descends steeply for approximately 900 vertical feet

**TIME:** Allow 3½ hours which includes time at the lake.

**HISTORY:** Named for the Soda Spring charged with carbon dioxide gas at the southeast corner of the lake.

**AUTHOR'S** The hike to Soda Lake is probably the last area to be free of snow
**COMMENTS:** I took the hike in September (following a heavy snow year) and th
wildflowers were just coming into bloom. This is a good hike to
take in late summer, after the bloom is off the rose, so to speak, i
lower elevations.

Soda Lake is not part of the Lassen Park trail system. It does not have a main-
tained trail. Sections of the hike have a discernible footpath, but most of the
hike is over open ground. The hike is not recommended for novice hikers or
small children unless on a hike conducted by the Park Service. Even though the
hike is only approximately 2.0 miles one way, there is a long steep climb out
with no engineered trail to follow. The hike starts on a discernible footpath up a
natural draw to the west of the trail to Lassen Peak. The path swings westerly to
the south of Eagle Peak in a gradual ascent. It proceeds in a northwesterly direc
tion in a draw between Eagle Peak to the north and Ski Heil Peak to the south.
There is another draw from the southwest side of Eagle Peak proceeding to the
southwest and Pot Hole Meadows comes into view. You descend all the way to
Soda Lake some 900 vertical feet, so if you have any second thoughts about
continuing, now is the time to turn back.

Vulcan's Castle is to the right (north). You must stay left of Vulcan's Castle.
There is a huge area of talus (rock slide) in this area. Many wildflowers make
their appearance as you descend. Silverleaf Lupine, Knot Weed, Pussy Toes,
Pussy Paws, Owls Clover, Bog Kalmia, Asters, and Mountain Heather are the
most common. Upon reaching Pot Hole Meadows, the flowers that like it wet
do their thing, including: Marsh Marigold, Cinquefoil, Senecio, Monkey Flower,

Queen Anne's Lace, Arrow Leaf Groundsel, and Shooting Stars.

Following the stream descending out of the west side of Pot Hole Meadows, Soda Lake can be seen at the west side of a second meadow. The springs at the southwest side of Soda Lake have a soda taste, from which the lake derives its name. The Soda Springs have a rust colored bottom. There is little or no carbonation to the water. On returning, proceed around the lake, crossing the outlet on the north side. (From here it's possible to hike to Manzanita Lake picking up the trail at the end of Manzanita Creek, but there is no established trail.) It's well worth the walk around the lake for scenic views. There is a long steep climb out on the return.

# 9 Paradise Meadow
*From Park Road via Terrace Lake Trail*

**TRAILHEAD:** Guide marker #27

**FEATURES:** Meadows, wildflowers, stream

**DISTANCE:** 1.6 miles (2.6 km) one way

**TIME:** Allow 2 to 2½ hours

8000'
7600'  PARADISE MEADOW
7200'
6800'
MILES  .5  1.0  1.5  2.0

**HISTORY:** *Paradise Meadow* is named because of the meadow's pleasant beauty with its beautiful wildflowers.

**AUTHOR'S COMMENTS:** When planning a hike to Paradise Meadow, allow enough time to spend at the meadow. Its beauty provides an intimacy that makes it hard to leave. Also, the return hike, because of its unbroken ascent, requires most people to rest frequently and is difficult for small children. Paradise Meadow from guide marker #27 is probably one of the last trails in the Park free of snow. However, it is also accessible from the trailhead at guide marker #42 which opens up much earlier. Another way to plan this hike is to arrange for transportation at guide marker #42 and start at marker #27 for a three mile hike all downhill.

Initially, the trail is the same as the trail to Terrace, Shadow, and Cliff Lakes. After .2 of a mile, the trail forks with the trail to Paradise Meadows going left 1.4 miles. It is well marked. The trail descends at a moderate rate all the way to Paradise Meadow. At the start, the forest is entirely Mountain Hemlock. There are examples of glacier polish with striations on the rocks. Lassen Peak is in view to the left (west). Also, there are many varieties of birds inhabiting this area. As the trail descends, Red Fir and Western White Pine join the forest. The ground cover, though sparse for the first mile or so with scattered Lupine, continues to

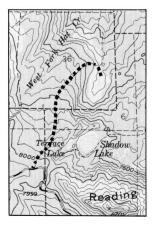

become more verdant.

After approximately 1.5 miles, the trail crosses the stream flowing out of Paradise Meadow and makes a sharp turn to the right (south). The wildflowers are profuse. The trail follows the stream for approximately .1 of a mile to the meadow. Most of the wildflowers are concentrated on the west side of the meadow on the other side of the stream. The author suggests that rather than cross the stream at the trail marker, take a footpath on the west side of the stream for the .1 of a mile south to the meadow and avoid wading across it at the meadow. Reading Peak is the prominent peak to the forefront which adds the perfect capping for a beautiful mountain meadow abundant with a dozen or so varieties of wildflowers. The return, though relatively short, is a steady tiring climb.

# 10 Southwest Campground

*Park Road (road guide #30) to Southwest Campground via Cold Boiling and Crumbaugh Lakes, Conard Meadows and Mill Creek Falls*

**TRAILHEAD:** Kings Creek Picnic Area, Road sign #30

**FEATURES:** Lakes, forest, waterfalls, wildflowers

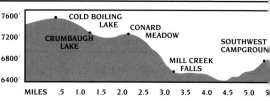

**DISTANCE:** Cold Boiling Lake .7 of a mile (1.1 km), Crumbaugh Lake 1.2 miles

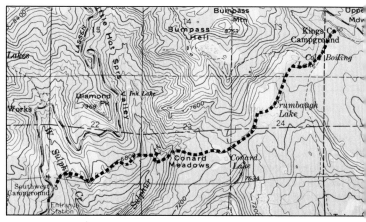

(1.9 km), Conard Meadows 2,6 miles (4.2 km), Mill Creek Falls 3.4 miles (5.5 km), Southwest Campground 5.1 miles (8.2 km) one way.

**TIME:** 3 1/2 to 4 hours: Cold Boiling Lake 1/2 hour, Crumbaugh Lake 3/4 hour, Conard Meadows 1 1/2 hours, Mill Creek Falls 2 hours, Southwest 3 hours.

**HISTORY:** *Cold Boiling Lake* was named "Cold" to distinguish it from the hydrothermal areas that frequent the Park. "Boiling" comes from the bubbling carbon dioxide gas at the north edge of the lake. *Crumbaugh Lake* is named after Peter C. Crumbaugh, a native of Maryland who came to Red Bluff in 1860 and grazed sheep in the vicinity of the lake.

---

**AUTHOR'S COMMENTS:** It is suggested you park your car at the Southwest Campground, obtain a ride to Kings Creek picnic area, and hike back to your car. An alternative is to return to Kings Creek picnic area after reaching Mill Creek Falls. This would be a hike of 6.8 miles — allow 3 1/2 to 4 hours.

---

After a rise, the trail levels and proceeds to Cold Boiling Lake. The forest is sparse Mountain Hemlock, Western White Pine, Lodgepole Pine and Red Fir. Wildflowers are mainly Lupine. At Cold Boiling Lake, the trail forks to the left to Crumbaugh Lake, and to the right to Bumpass Hell. The trail skirts the left side of the meadow. There are abundant wildflowers including Pennyroyal, Mountain Heather, Buttercups, Lewis Monkey Flower, Corn and Leopard Lily, Aster, Queen Anne's Lace, Large Leaf Lupine on marshy spots, and Silverleaf Lupine where it's dry. From Cold Boiling Lake, the trail descends through Red Fir and Mountain Hemlock to Crumbaugh Lake.

Arriving at Crumbaugh Lake, there is a beautiful view of Mt. Conard to the south. The main trail goes around the west or right side of the lake. However, you can walk around the lake starting on the east and pick up the trail on the west after circling most of the lake. The best swimming is on a gravel bar on the west side. Leaving the lake, the trail rises gradually for .2 of a mile, levels for .4 of a mile through a beautiful forest of Red Fir and Hemlock with wildflowers. This section of forest is one of the best in the park. The trail then descends gradually into Conard Meadows. Brokeoff and Diller Mountains are visible ahead.

One tenth of a mile past the trail marker indicating Mill Creek Falls, .7 of a mile, the trail crosses a cold mountain stream coming out of Conard Meadows. It's a perfect spot to stop and refresh oneself, refill the canteen and enjoy the wildflowers and scenery, including a view to the right of a rock that looks like Pilot Pinnacle but is not. From here, the trail descends rapidly to Mill Creek Falls.

Mill Creek Falls are difficult to see until you have crossed East Sulphur Creek. There are wildflowers including Penstemon just above the falls. After crossing the creek, the trail ascends moderately until you are out of the canyon, where there is an excellent view of the falls. The trail proceeds down through grassy meadows and Fir trees with views of Brokeoff and Mt. Diller. The trail descends to West Sulphur Creek and then ascends to the Southwest Campground.

# 11 Twin Meadows

*From Park Road*

**TRAILHEAD:** Kings Creek picnic area, sign post #30

**FEATURES:** Interesting rock formations, wildflowers, forest, meadows and streams.

**DISTANCE:** 2.3 miles (3.8 km) one way

**TIME:** 2½ to 3 hours

**WILDLIFE:** Birds (Clark's Nutcracker), deer

*[Elevation profile: 7600', 7200', 6800', 6400'; MILES .5 1.0 1.5 2.0 2.5 3.; TWIN MEADOWS]*

**HISTORY:** Twin Meadows: So named because of a topographic construction resulting from a low ridge projecting into the meadow dividing the meadow in half.

The trail is the same as the trail to Cold Boiling Lake, Crumbaugh Lake, Conard Meadows and Mill Creek Falls at the beginning. After an initial rise, the trail levels and after .4 of a mile, the trail to Twin Meadows forks to the left. It is well-marked. Immediately after the fork, there is a nice stand of Red Fir. Ground cover at this point is Lupine and other wild flowers including Indian Paint Brush. The trail follows a gully which was made by a glacier. Also on the left are rock formations. The forest is Mountain Hemlock, Western White Pine, Red Fir and Lodgepole Pine. The trail proceeds in a southerly direction and with a gradual descent. Seven tenths of a mile from the fork, the forest opens and there is a good view of Mt. Conard. Ground cover is Pinemat Manzanita which provides a certain beauty. Generally the forest is not as inspiring as most in the Park. Twin Meadows is fed by two forks of the north arm of Rice Creek, and is abundant in wildflowers. On the northeast corner of the Lower Meadow, there is an old roofless log cabin. The trail continues on to Growler Hot Springs and Child's Meadows which are outside the Park.

# 12 Sifford Lakes
*Via Bench Lake and Kings Creek Falls*

**TRAILHEAD:** Kings Creek, where it crosses the Park road — Marker #32 (parking lot on the north side; turnouts on the south side)

**FEATURES:** Wildflowers, lakes, spectacular views of Warner Valley including Devils Kitchen, forests and cliffs

**DISTANCE:** 2.1 miles (3.4 km) to Sifford Lakes and an additional .7 of a mile (1.1 km) for return via Bench Lake and Kings Creek Falls (see map for Hike 15)

**TIME:** 2½ to 3 hours. Add 1/2 hour for return via Bench Lake and Kings Creek Falls

**HISTORY:** Named after Alex Sifford, who with his family managed and owned the Drakesbad Resort for many years.

The trail to Sifford Lakes and Kings Creek Falls is the same at the start. The trail parallels Kings Creek with a gradual descent. After .4 of a mile, the trail forks with the left fork going to Kings Creek Falls and the right to Sifford Lakes. After 1.7 miles from the beginning, the trail again forks with the right going to Sifford Lakes, and the left to Drakesbad. After a short rise, you come to the first lake at elevation 7,200 feet. The lake provides excellent swimming by mid-summer with the best entrance on the southwest side. Continuing past the lake, there are a series of magnificent cliffs with a spectacular view of Warner Valley. Devils Kitchen is in prominent view. Mt. Harkness and Lake Almanor can be seen to the east and southeast respectively. Care should be taken as there is approximately a 1,000 foot vertical fall from the edge.

From the south side of the first lake, the trail swings west with a steep ascent for approximately .2 of a mile to the second lake. The third and fourth lakes are nearby. Return the same way, or return to the trail to Drakesbad and continue on it for a steep descent for .3 of a mile to the turn-off to Bench Lake. From the fork, the trail is level for .3 of a mile. Bench Lake is more like a pond, and it dries up in dry years. From the lake, the trail ascends a ridge, then descends to a log bridge over Kings Creek. The trail joins the Kings Creek Falls trail just above Kings Creek Falls with a return of 1.1 miles.

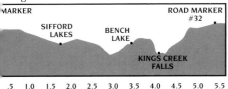

MARKER                            ROAD MARKER
#32

SIFFORD
LAKES           BENCH
LAKE

KINGS CREEK
FALLS

.5   1.0   1.5   2.0   2.5   3.0   3.5   4.0   4.5   5.0   5.5

# 13 Paradise Meadow

*From the Park Road (guide marker #42) and Return*

**TRAILHEAD:** Guide marker #42

**FEATURES:** Wildflowers, meadow, forest, stream

**DISTANCE:** Paradise Meadow 1.4 miles (2.2 km), Park Road 2.8 miles (4.5 km), Terrace Lake 3.0 miles (4.8 km)

**TIME:** Allow 2 to 2½ hours

**WILDLIFE:** Deer, eagle

**HISTORY:** *Paradise Meadow* is named because of the meadow's pleasant beauty with its beautiful wildflowers.

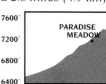

**AUTHOR'S COMMENTS:** This hike is much easier starting at guide marker #27 and hiking downhill all the way. The total distance is about the same as starting at guide post #42 and returning. This hike in most years is conducted by the Park Service, called "Hike to Paradise." It is well worth it if you can fit it into your schedule. The hike to Paradise Meadow is one of the best wildflower hikes in the Park. The best time is usually mid-July to early August.

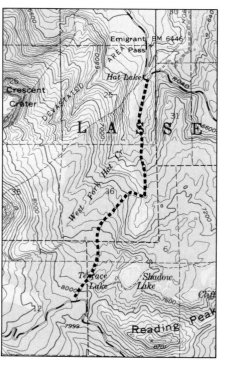

The trail initially is level through an open Lodgepole Pine forest, and affords good views of Lassen Peak to the right and Reading Peak to the forefront. After .1 of a mile, the trail starts a gradual ascent, and after another .2 of a mile, the trail steepens and Red and White Fir start replacing the Lodgepole Pine. The trail crosses a series of intermittent streams abundant in wildflowers. As the trail steepens, Western White Pine replaces the Lodgepole Pine. The trail parallels the east fork of Hat Creek flowing out of Paradise Meadow. The steep trail levels for .1 of a mile to the trail marker sign with Paradise Meadow straight ahead. Terrace Lake 1.4 miles, Park Road 1.5 miles, Shadow Lake 1.7 miles and Summit Lake 5.0 miles to the right. In the author's opinion, it's best to cross the creek here and follow the footpath to Paradise Meadow, as most of the wildflowers in the meadow are on the west side of the creek.

# 4 Hat Lake to Soap L.

*Via Badger Flat and Return*

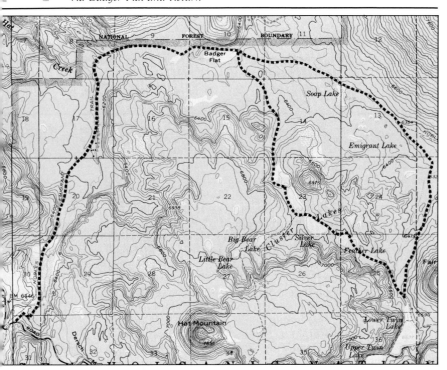

**TRAILHEAD:** Sign Marker #41

**FEATURES:** Nobles Emigrant Trail, forest, lake

**DISTANCE:** Badger Flat 6.0 miles (9.7 km), Soap Lake 7.5 miles (12.2 km), Lower Twin Lake Trail Junction 8.6 miles (13.9 km), return 17.2 miles (27.9 km)

**TIME:** Allow 4½ hours one way

**WILDLIFE:** Deer, hawk

**HISTORY:** *Hat Lake* is named after the west fork of Hat Creek. It was dammed by the mud flow of Lassen's May 19, 1915 eruptions.
*Badger Flat* was named for badgers who lived there, and originally called "Pine Meadows" in the 1850's. In 1884, it was called "Booker Flat" after John R. Booker, a freighter, who used the meadows as a resting place enroute to Oregon. This parcel was patented October 30, 1907 by Horace Herbert, and his sons Andy and Fred grazed cattle until they sold it to Hugh Addington in 1946. It was purchased by the federal government in 1948.

29

**AUTHOR'S**   Distances measured on the trail marker signs are the distances be-
**COMMENTS:**  tween signs, and not necessarily the distances between the places.
               This hike is not recommended as a hike with a return be-
cause of its distance (17.2 miles), but is described rather for backpackers going from the Park road to Lower Twin or Butte Lakes. It
is an alternative for starting at the more popular Summit Lake for
hikers interested in the Nobles Emigrant Trail. It is also one way to
hike the Pacific Crest Trail from north to south within the Park
boundaries. The portion of the trail to Butte Lake and also to
Lower Twin Lake is discussed on page 62, describing the hike from
"Butte Lake to Lower Twin Lake via the Nobles Emigrant Trail,
return via Rainbow Lake."

There is no trail sign, but the trail follows the road at the locked gate. The road
is in fact the Nobles Emigrant Trail. The trail descends for .4 of a mile through
an open forest of Red Fir, Lodgepole Pine, and Aspen where it crosses Hat
Creek. After crossing Hat Creek, the trail levels through an uninspiring dense forest of Lodgepole Pine. After 1.2 miles, the forest opens briefly, thus providing
good views of Lassen Peak to the rear. Six tenths of a mile further, there are
talus slopes on the left. One mile further, the trail forks with the right-hand trail
going to a cabin. Three miles from the start, the trail crosses Hat Creek with a
trail marker sign: Badger Flat 3.0 miles (4.8 km), Cluster Lake 5.1 miles (8.2 km),
Cinder Cone 8.7 miles (14.0 km), Butte Lake 9.7 miles (15.6 km). At the time of
writing, there is no bridge across Hat Creek. However, the bottom is smooth and
easily crossed in bare feet.

Nine tenths of a mile from the trail marker sign, the trail forks into a
beautiful stand of Jeffrey Pine with the left-hand trail a fire road which joins the
Pacific Crest Trail in .5 of a mile at the Park's northern boundary. Proceeding to
the right .2 of a mile further, the trail starts a moderate rise through a forest of
outstanding White Fir, Jeffrey and Ponderosa Pine. Two tenths of a mile further,
the trail joins the Pacific Crest Trail, where it forks to the left (north). At the time
of writing, the sign post was all that was left of the sign. There is a Pacific Crest
Trail tag nailed to a Jeffrey Pine. After .3 of a mile further, the trail levels, and the
forest goes back to a repetitious stand of Lodgepole Pine. Ground cover is predominately Bloomers Goldenbush. Two tenths of a mile before the trail junction,
Badger Flat is visible to the right.

At the Badger Flat trail junction, Hat Lake back 6.1 miles (9.7 km), straight
ahead Butte Lake 6.6 miles (10.6 km), to the right (south) Cluster Lake 2.0 miles
(3.3 km), Big Bear Lake 3.2 miles (5.1 km), Lower Twin Lake 5.0 miles (8.0 km),
Summit Lake 6.8 miles (10.9 km). Continuing straight ahead, the trail ascends
moderately through the continuing forest of mostly Lodgepole Pine for .2 of a
mile, then becomes fairly level. It continues in an easterly direction for 1.3 miles
further to Soap Lake on the right (south). In another 1.1 miles, there is a trail
junction with Lower Twin Lake to the right (south) 2.8 miles (4.4 km). Ahead is
Cinder Cone 3.1 miles (5.0 km) and Badger Flat to the rear 2.6 miles (4.1 km).

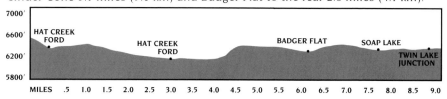

# 5 Kings Creek Falls

*From Park Road and Return*

**TRAILHEAD:** Kings Creek where it crosses the Park road (Marker #32). There are turn-outs on both side of the road.

**FEATURES:** Wildflowers, falls, forest

**DISTANCE:** 1.2 miles (1.9 km) one way via footpath, 1.5 miles (2.4 km) via horse trail

**TIME:** Allow 2 hours

**HISTORY:** Kings Creek Falls named after James M. King who ran horses in the area during the summer.

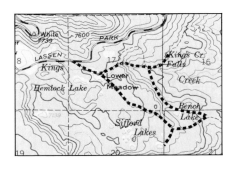

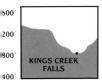

In the beginning, the trail to Kings Creek Falls and Sifford Lakes is the same, paralleling Kings Creek with a gradual descent for .4 of a mile, whereupon it forks. The right fork goes to Sifford Lakes and Drakesbad, and the left to Kings Creek Falls. The trail continues its descent through a forest of predominately Lodgepole Pine, Mountain Hemlock, and Red Fir. There's another fork with the horse trail going to the left .8 of a mile, and to the right, the foot trail down the cascades .5 of a mile. Straight ahead .1 of a mile is the Cascade View, well worth the short detour. The foot trail

down the edge is a "watch your step" one, and if you have fear of heights or a balance problem, the horse trail would be a better choice. Wildflowers include Aster, Lupine, Paint Brush, and Sulphur Flower.

Two tenths of a mile from the Falls, the horse trail rejoins the foot trail. A short distance past here, there is another trail junction with the fork to the right going to Bench Lake .6 of a mile, and the trail junction to Warner Valley 1.0 miles. The trail continues its descent to the Falls. The Falls are 50 feet high, second only to Mill Creek Falls in height. They should be photographed early in the day, prior to 1:00 pm as they are in shadows in the afternoon. The Falls as well as the Cascades are quite beautiful — sparkling as the waters tumble down the rock cliffs.

# 16 Manzanita Lake

*Trails from Manzanita Lake Campground area to Reflection Lake*

**TRAILHEAD:** Anywhere around the lake

**FEATURES:** Wildlife, lake, views

**DISTANCE:** .6 of a mile (1.0 km)

**TIME:** 1/2 hour or less

**TOPOGRAPHY:** Mostly level

**WILDLIFE:** Geese and ducks

**HISTORY:** Named for the smoothness of its waters. The west end of the Lake affords beautiful reflections of both Lassen Peak and Chaos Crags. Originally patented by William K. Coffey and John E. Stockton in the early 1880's. It was called Little Manzanita Lake and also Mud Lake. Eventually purchased by Mr. B. F. Loomis, and during this period called Stockton Lake after its former co-owner.

One tenth of a mile south of trail marker #65, across from the Loomis Museum is the trailhead for Lily Pond Trail, which is a self-guiding nature trail. It serves as a portion of the trail around the north shore of Reflection Lake. The lake is aptly named affording views of Lassen Peak and Chaos Crags reflecting in its waters. There are ducks and geese (Canadian honkers) inhabiting the lake.

# 17 Manzanita Lake

*Campground Area*

**TRAILHEAD:** Anywhere around the lake

**FEATURES:** Lake, views, wildlife, wildflowers, boating, fishing

**DISTANCE:** 1.5 miles (2.4 km)

**TIME:** 1 hour

**TOPOGRAPHY:** Level

**HISTORY:** Manzanita Lake takes its name from the Green Leaf Manzanita which is abundant in the nearby Manzanita chutes. Manzanita means in Spanish small apple, which aptly describes the small tart fruit that the shrub bears. Manzanita Lake was first owned by Burton L. Smith, who sold it to the Northern California Power Company in 1906. At this time, the company enlarged the lake by constructing a small earth-filled dam. In 1919, the Northern California Power Company sold it to the Pacific Gas and Electric

Company which in turn sold it to the federal government.

**AUTHOR'S**    Manzanita Lake has an excellent campground. A good time to take
**COMMENTS:**    this hike is after dinner and before the evening Ranger program.

This hike around Manzanita Lake is a photographer's paradise. The classic views of Lassen Peak seen on calendars and posters throughout the world are from the north and west shores. The early evening probably provides the best time for pictures as the sun is directly on Lassen Peak and the wind almost always dies so that the reflection is not rippled. The entire trail around the lake provides excellent views which combine with ducks, geese, and wildflowers floating in the lake to provide a feeling of tranquility. Behind the Ranger Station toward the lake, there is paved parking, and to the south, a boat launch. Power boats are prohibited. Fishing is allowed on the lake but restricted on Manzanita Creek leading into the lake. Fishing is catch and release. Fishing tackle, supplies and park literature are available at the store south of the Ranger Station.

# 8 Manzanita Lake
*Campground Area to Chaos Crags and Crags Lake*

**TRAILHEAD:**    On the road to Manzanita Campground approximately .1 of a mile
from the main park road within 100 feet of Manzanita Creek.

**FEATURES:**    Forest, flowers, rock slide

33

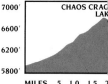

**DISTANCE:**  1.8 miles one way (2.9 km)

**TIME:**  Allow 2½ hours

**HISTORY:**  Named after Chaos Jumbles at the north base of the Crags. Chaos Jumbles named in 1937, was previously called Chaos Lava Beds.

---

**AUTHOR'S COMMENTS:**  This is one of those hikes that isn't so much what you see when you get there, as what you see while getting there. The forest and the views along the way provide the enjoyment.

---

The first part of the trail parallels Manzanita Creek on its east side. It has a gradual climb in an open forest of Jeffrey and Sugar Pine. As the trail gains elevation the forest thickens with many beautiful specimens of Red and White Fir. Some of the trees have blackened trunks, indicating a fire many years ago. In approximately .3 of a mile, the trail swings away from Manzanita Creek, and descends through a thick Fir forest. It levels, and then ascends after .1 of a mile. After approximately .7 of a mile from the beginning, evidence of the famous rock slide of about 300 years ago is quite evident. The chance of another rock slide occurring is the reason for the closing of the Manzanita Lake concession and park facilities in 1974. There are very few wildflowers along the trail. Approximately 1.5 miles from the beginning, the ground cover becomes Green Leaf (large) and Pinemat Manzanita (small) which offers an interesting contrast. For the last .1 of a mile, the trail descends steeply into Chaos Crags Lake. The lake is really a pond and dries up in most summers. However, the view of Chaos Crags is excellent.

# 19 Manzanita Creek
*Manzanita Lake Campground Area*

**TRAILHEAD:**  South end of Manzanita Campground near the exit of Loop F

**FEATURES:**  Forest, wildflowers, mountain meadows, and creek

**DISTANCE:**  3.5 miles (5.7 km) one way

**TIME:**  3½ to 4 hours

**HISTORY:**  Manzanita Creek is named after Manzanita Lake which it flows into and out of.

---

The trail starts its steady ascent up a fire road, which is chained at the start. The ground is sparsely covered with Green Leaf Manzanita. The forest is mostly Jeffrey Pine, White and Red Fir. The trail proceeds in a southeasterly direction with Lassen Peak visible to the forefront, and Chaos Crags to the east. After .5 of a mile, the forest improves with many large majestic trees as well as small symmetrically shaped Red and White Fir, which Christmas tree cutters refer to as a jackpot area. In addition to being marked by customary yellow discs, the trail is

34                                                                      Hiking Trails of Lassen

so marked by red trail markers with a yellow vertical line in the center. It's virtually impossible to lose the trail. The trail continues its steady climb which makes for easy walking, and Pinemat Manzanita and Blue Penstemon become the ground cover. After a little over a mile, Loomis Peak becomes visible to the south. The trail levels and becomes profuse with many wildflowers including Silver Leaf Lupine, Pennyroyal, Fireweed, Lewis Monkey Flower, and Indian Paint Brush. After approximately 1.6 miles, the trail joins and parallels Manzanita Creek and .1 of a mile further, it crosses the creek. This provides a nice place to refill your canteen with the ice cold water from the creek. After crossing the creek, the trail resumes its relentless gradual ascent. From the start

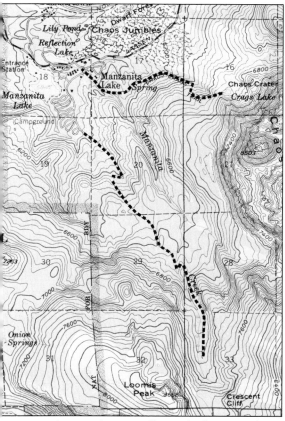

proximately 2.3 miles Mt. Diller and Pilot Pinnacle are visible to the south, southest. In another .4 of a mile, the trail enters a mountain meadow abundant with ldflowers, and crosses ice cold rivulets of water feeding Manzanita Creek. The trail adually peters out in the meadow. There are animal trails leading up Crescent iff for those wishing to extend the hike to Soda Lake.

# 20 Summit Lake
*Summit Lake to Cluster Lakes and return via Lower and Upper Twin and Echo Lake with detour to Badger Flat*

**TRAILHEAD:** Northeast side of Summit Lake

**FEATURES:** Lakes, swimming, forests, flowers, and views

**DISTANCE:** Little Bear Lake 3.2 miles (5.1 km), Big Bear Lake 3.5 miles (5.7 km), Cluster Lake 4.2 miles (6.7 km), Lower Twin Lake 6.6 miles (10.6 km), Upper Twin Lake 7.1 miles (11.4 km), Echo Lake 9.0 miles (14.5 km), Summit Lake 10.7 miles (17.3 km). Add 5.2 miles for detour to Badger Flat.

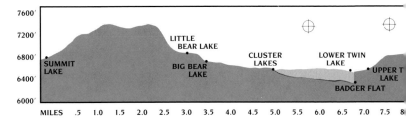

| 7600' | | | | | | | | | | | | | | | | |
| 7200' | | | | | | | ⊕ | | | ⊕ | | | | | |
| 6800' | | | LITTLE BEAR LAKE | | | CLUSTER LAKES | | LOWER TWIN LAKE | | | | | | | |
| SUMMIT LAKE | | | | BIG BEAR LAKE | | | | | | UPPER T LAKE | | | | | |
| 6400' | | | | | | | | | BADGER FLAT | | | | | | |
| 6000' | | | | | | | | | | | | | | | | |
| MILES | .5 | 1.0 | 1.5 | 2.0 | 2.5 | 3.0 | 3.5 | 4.0 | 4.5 | 5.0 | 5.5 | 6.0 | 6.5 | 7.0 | 7.5 | 8 |

**TIME:** Allow 6 hours plus extra time for swimming. Add 2 hours for detour to Badger Flat.

**HISTORY:** *Cluster Lakes:* Applies to a series of six lakes of which three are named — Cluster Lake, Silver Lake and Feather Lake.
*Lower and Upper Twin Lakes:* The name comes from the fact that these two adjacent lakes are of similar character, origin, and size, and are at somewhat different levels, 6575 feet and 6540 feet. They have also been called "Twin Lakes" by a surveyor, Lt. S. E. Tillman Also named in the official Shasta County map of 1884 as "Bee Lake" and in 1922 as "Busy Bee Lake."

**AUTHOR'S COMMENTS:** Start with full canteen (unless you drink lake water, which is not recommended). This hike offers excellent swimming, forests, and beautiful lakes. It is best taken in mid-August on a warm day. The author does not necessarily recommend the detour to Badger Flat as this time might be best spent swimming, or enjoying the beaut

The trail ascends at a moderate to steep climb for approximately .8 of a mile through an open Red Fir forest with a scattering of Mountain Hemlock, Western White and Lodgepole Pine. Ground cover is sparse, mainly Pinemat Manzanita contrasting interestingly with Greenleaf Manzanita and some Lupine. As the trail climbs Lassen Peak, Chaos Crags and Reading Peak can be observed to the west (behind you). The trail levels for approximatel .1 of a mile when it comes to the trail junction to Little Bear Lake 2.4 miles (3.8 km), Big Bear Lake 2.7 miles (4.4 km), Cluster Lakes 3.3 miles (5.3 km) and Badger Flat 5.9 miles (9.6 km) forking left (north). From the trail junction, the trail is level and then starts a gradual ascent through a pleasant open Fir forest with a carpet of Pinemat Manzanita. The trail descends to an unnamed lake we will call Lake George. The best entry for swimming is on its north side. Approximately 1.0 miles of descent from Lake George is Little Bear Lake. The best swimming is also on the north side. There are camp sites all around the lake.

The trail follows the eastern shore and swings east for approximately .3 of a mile to Big Bear Lake. It continues around the southeast side of the lake in a northeasterly direction. Approximately .3 of a mile from Big Bear Lake, there is another outstanding stand of Red Fir and Western White Pine. In .2 of a mile, th

trail forks again with Badger Flat 2.6 miles left (north), and to the right (south), Lower Twin Lake 2.4 miles. Proceeding to Badger Flat, the trail is mostly level with a few gradual descents. It travels in a northerly direction through a Fir forest. It proceeds along the western edge of Cluster Lake and then passes several mostly dried up lakes which have seen better days. The ground is very porous and dry with sparse ground cover. Badger Flat is a large meadow with water running through it, and there are places to camp.

This trail is a junction joining the Pacific Crest Trail, Hat Lake 6.1 miles left (west), Butte Lake 6.6 miles right (east). Returning back 2.6 miles to the original trail junction to Badger Flat, the trail proceeds in a southerly direction, and in .2 of a mile past the junction, there is a lake with a silver cast, hence the name Silver Lake. The trail follows its eastern edge. There are wildflowers and cool grassy spots to rest or swim. Another .3 of a mile of level terrain brings Feather Lake. This lake has a turquoise color, and one has to be impressed with the individual beauty of each lake as though they were trying in their own unique way to literally outshine their neighbor.

Another mile or so is the junction of the Soap Lake Emigrant Trail. In approximately .1 of a mile, the trail goes past an old C.C.C. cabin on the left, and then joins the north side of Lower Twin Lake. It swings towards the lake and around the right (north) side. The best swimming is at this point. The trail then

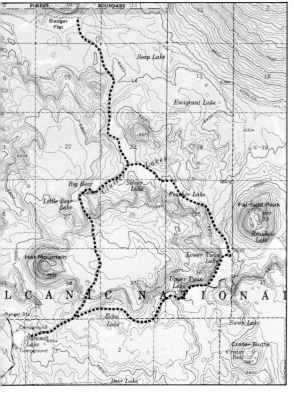

continues a short distance to Upper Twin Lake, and travels on its north bank. It climbs out of Upper Twin Lake and then through a series of rises, and levels to Echo Lake. Both Echo and Upper Twin Lake have good swimming, but Echo Lake is much colder. Then, there is a long remembered steep climb out of Echo Lake back to the ridge where the trail started. The trail rejoins the trail marker at the junction to Little and Big Bear lakes completing the loop, and then returns to the trailhead.

# 21 Summit Lake

*Summit Lake to Corral Meadow to Upper and Lower Twin Lake via Grassy Swale and return via Echo Lake*

**TRAILHEAD:** Southeast corner of Loop F, south section of Summit Lake Campground

**FEATURES:** Wildlife, flowers, lakes, swimming, forest, views, solitude

**DISTANCE:** Corral Meadow 2.4 miles (3.9 km), Lower Twin Lake 7.0 miles (11.3 km), Upper Twin Lake 7.5 miles (12.2 km), Echo Lake 9.4 mile (15.2 km), return to Summit Lake 11.1 miles (18.0 km)

**TIME:** Allow 6½ hours plus additional time for swimming

**WILDLIFE:** Deer, bear

**HISTORY:** *Corral Meadow:* Named after a log corral built by a Frenchman, George La Pie, a "long time ago."
*Grassy Swale* derives its name from the designation "Grassy Lake," which was formerly used for Horseshoe Lake. It is an irregular meadow-like area appro...mately three miles long; the upper part joins a meadow adjacent to Horseshoe Lake. "Swale" is also descriptive meaning a piece of meadow, marshy or rank with vegetation.
*Lower and Upper Twin Echo Lake:* See "History" as described in the hike "Summit to Cluster Lakes and return via Lower and Upper Twin and Echo Lake," page 35.

**AUTHOR'S COMMENTS:** Water is available for first half of hike only.

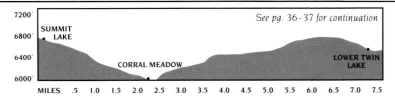

See pg. 36-37 for continuation

Approximately .1 of a mile from the start, there is a huge Western White Pine on the left which measures approximately 25 feet in circumference. The trail is on a gradual descent through a forest of Western White Pine and Red Fir. Ground cover initially is wet and grassy as the trail parallels Summit Lake Creek. Wildflowers inhabit this area consisting of mostly Queen Anne's Lace. Deer are quite common near Summit Lake and I saw a buck within .1 of a mile of the campground. In a little over a mile, the trail nears a cold mountain stream, a tributary of Kings Creek. It is a good place to fill your canteen. It has the usual wildflowers associated with wet places. Approximately 1.6 miles from the start of the hike, there is an excellent place to camp. It is level, next to water, and out of hearing of all the crying children at Summit Lake (just barely). One tenth of a mile further, the trail joins with the trail to Kings Creek Meadows 3.3 miles, Kings Creek Falls 2.2 miles with Corral Meadow .7 of a mile ahead.

One tenth of a mile further from the trail junction, the trail crosses Kings Creek, then parallels it on its west side.

Approximately .2 of a mile after crossing Kings Creek, there are some good camping spots and .2 of a mile further, the falls are visible to the left where Grassy Swale Creek joins Kings Creek. One tenth of a mile further the trail arrives at Corral Meadow with trail junction Warner Valley ahead 2.4 miles and Kelly Camp ahead 4.0 miles. To the left is Horseshoe Lake 4.5 miles, Lower Twin Lake 4.6 miles, Cinder Cone 8.8 miles, and Butte Lake 10.1 miles. At this point, we join the Pacific Crest Trail. The trail switches back and recrosses Kings Creek. The trail starts a steep ascent out of the Kings Creek drainage paralleling Grassy Swale Creek on its south side. The trail continues with a gradual ascent. The forest is not spectacular but is pleasant. The trail then crosses a mountain meadow and wild lilac appear.

Approximately 1.2 miles from the last trail junction, the trail crosses Grassy Swale Creek with many wildflowers present. The trail continues to parallel the creek and at this point a bear came across the meadow within 30 feet of the author. There is no picture because the author got buck (or rather bear fever) and didn't have his telephoto adjusted, and the bear was gone. The trail remains level and is peaceful with many birds and deer.

Two and four tenths miles from Corral Meadow, the trail forks with Horseshoe Lake 2.0 miles to the right (south), Lower Twin Lake 2.2 miles, Cinder Cone 4.4 miles and Butte Lake 4.7 miles to the left (north). After .2 of a mile, there is a good display of the wildflowers that like it dry: Pussy Paws, Blue Penstemon, Lupine, Skyrocket Gilia, and Indian Paint Brush. The trail swings away from the creek in a

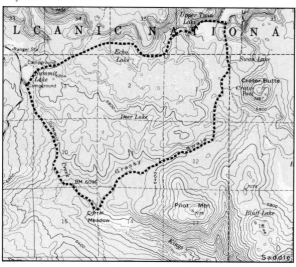

northerly direction. After approximately .8 of a mile from the Horseshoe Lake fork, the forest changes into Lodgepole Pine with the soil quite porous and dry. One and three tenths miles from the Horseshoe Lake fork, the Horseshoe Lake loop rejoins with Horseshoe Lake 2.2 miles to the right, and Lower Twin Lake .9 of a mile ahead. At this trail junction is an outstanding stand of Red Fir. Three tenths of a mile further, Swan Lake appears to the right. The trail joins at Lower Twin Lakes with the trails to Upper Twin Lake .5 of a mile and Summit Lake 4.1 miles to the left (west). To the right (along the Pacific Crest Trail) Snag Lake 3.0 miles, Cinder Cone 4.2 miles, Badger Flat 5.4 miles, and Butte Lake 5.5 miles. The level trail proceeds around the south side of Lower Twin Lake in a westerly direction. The best swimming is on the other side of the lake, and Fairfield Peak is in view to the north. The trail joins a trail on the north side of the lake, and

goes westerly for .1 of a mile to Upper Twin Lake. From this point, hikers are common, for this is the main route for backpackers from Summit Lake to Snag, Butte, Horseshoe and Juniper Lakes. So, modest skinny-dippers beware.

From Upper Twin Lake, there is a steep climb then the trail levels and has a series of climbs and levels. It passes several small lakelets and drops .1 of a mile into Echo Lake which is 1.5 miles from Upper Twin Lake. Echo Lake is just as pretty as its twin sisters, but smaller and much colder. From Echo Lakes the trail has a short rise, levels for .3 of a mile and then climbs steeply for what seems like forever actually only for .3 of a mile up the ridge. It levels and joins the trail junction to Little Bear Lake 2.4 miles, Big Bear Lake 2.7 miles, and Summit Lake .9 of a mile ahead. After .1 of a mile, the trail descends into Summit Lake. There are majestic views of Lassen Peak, Chaos Crags, and Reading Peak along the way. The trail joins the trailhead at the north end of Summit Lake and it is .3 of a mile south to the original trailhead.

*Golden-Mantled Ground Squirrel (Citellus lateralis)*

**DRAKESBAD HISTORY:**

*Named by Alex Sifford in 1900 when he purchased the property from Edward R. Drake. The "Bad" portion of the name comes from the German word for bath or spa; this is because there are hot springs free of the usual sulphuric and sulphurous acids, making them suitable for hot bathing. There is a possibility there were two tracts of land comprising Drakesbad, the other being owned by the Tom Malgin family. By 1881 the Malgins had developed open log conduit and a log bath house. In 1905 the area was also known as "Drake Springs." The Sifford family operated the Drakesbad Guest Ranch until 1958 when it was purchased by the Park Service. has been operated by the Park Concession ever since in much of the same manner. At the Drakesbad Guest Ranch there is a scrap book with a detailed history of the Guest Ranch from 1900 until its sale to the Park Service. Drakesbad Guest Ranch offers some important services to hikers and backpackers. First is a telephone for collect and credit card calls. Cold drinks, candy and trail mix are for sale. Meals are available provided you have a confirmed reservation. A nice hike is from Kings Creek to Drakesbad. Have someone meet you for dinner, and thus provide a ride back to your accommodations or camp. Park literature, including trail maps, is also for sale. The naturally heated pool is restricted to guests, but Dream Lake offers an alternative. Horses and horseback riding are available.*

**HISTORY:** *Warner Valley* named after a pioneer trapper who lived in the valley.

# Drakesbad

*Kelly Camp to Corral Meadow, return to Warner Valley Campground via Flatiron Ridge*

**TRAILHEAD:** One tenth of a mile west of the bridge and 1.9 miles toward Chester from the Ranger Station where the pavement starts, there is a dirt road going north past cabins on the right for .4 of a mile where the road ends.

**FEATURES:** Fishing, wildflowers, forest, panoramic views

**DISTANCE:** 3.8 miles (6.1 km) to Corral Meadow, 2.5 miles (4.0 km) Corral Meadow to Warner Valley Campground. Total of 6.3 miles (10.2 km)

**TIME:** 4 hours plus fishing time

**HISTORY:** Kelly Camp is named after Jim Kelly who homesteaded the head of Warner Valley just outside the park. Flatiron Ridge is a 3.5 mile long irregular plateau of andecite lava with a pointed apex terminating in Warner Valley. It was so named because of its shape by Jim Kelly.

**AUTHOR'S COMMENTS:** The hardest part of this hike is finding the trailhead. Even though the trail from Kelly Camp follows Kings Creek on the map, much of the time the creek is inaccessible. Therefore, for obtaining water or for fishing, do it when you can reach the stream easily. There is no water from Corral Meadow to Warner Valley Campground. It is my opinion that within the park boundaries, stream fishing should be limited to barbless artificial lures, flies, etc., and all fish returned to the stream. This would improve the fishing so that those wishing to learn fly-fishing would have a good chance of catching fish, which is really how to learn. Also, the author feels this restriction is more compatible with the Park's philosophy and not inconsistent with the rules which forbid hunting.

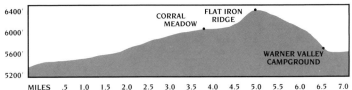

The trail begins on the east side of Kings Creek proceeding in a northerly direction. The trail has a gradual ascent and goes through a nice forest of mostly White Fir and Jeffrey Pine. After approximatley .5 of a mile, the trail joins the edge of the creek, and a rock slide is in view on its west side. The author fly-fished upstream for an hour starting here. Kings Creek has excellent fishing water and is good for fly-fishing with lots of open area and practically no brush. Fishing at this point was only fair (4 in one hour), however, it does not appear to be heavily fished. Along the trail, there is a yellow fungus about the size of abalone attached to some trees. There are some wildflowers including Skyrocket Gilia, Indian Paint Brush, Blue Penstemon. The trail continues through a beautiful fir forest consisting of mainly White Fir. After approximately 1.4 miles or so from the start, the trail crosses Kings Creek. Again, I tried fishing upstream and caught 9 in an hour, including rainbow, brook and brown trout. All fish were returned to the creek. It appears that the best fishing is from here up to within 1/2 mile of Corral Meadow. Corral Meadow is a popular camping spot and fished heavily within 1/2 mile or so.

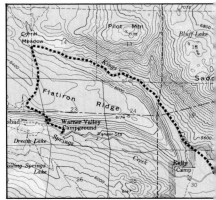

After leaving the creek, the trail ascends gradually and Red Fir and Western White Pine become more plentiful. Woodpeckers inhabit this area. Three and five tenths miles from the start, and .3 of a mile from Corral Meadow, the trail joins with the trail from Warner Valley Campground (the Pacific Crest Trail). At the trail junction, there is a beautiful stand of huge Red Fir trees. Corral Meadow is to Lassen's trails as Chicago is to railroads. Trails branch out to Summit, Lower Twin, Horseshoe Lakes as well as Kings Creek Falls and Drakesbad.

Returning .3 of a mile from Corral Meadow to the previously described trail junction, the trail forks to the right for Warner Valley Campground (2.2 miles). The trail rises moderately to steeply for .8 of a mile, then becomes level, traveling through a dense forest of Red and White Fir. It then descends gradually for .3 of a mile. When it levels, the forest is open and has a peaceful feel to it. One and five tenths miles from Corral Meadow, there is a trail junction with the trail to Sifford Lakes 2.3 miles, Kings Creek Falls 2.6 miles, and Kings Creek Meadows 3.6 miles. For the last mile, the trail descends into Warner Valley. There are majestic cliffs and a wonderful panorama of Warner Valley with the Drakesbad Guest Ranch visible on the Valley floor.

# 23 Drakesbad

*Drakesbad to Kings Creek via Sifford Lakes, return via Kings Creek Falls and Corral Meadow*

**TRAILHEAD:** Upper Warner Valley Campground

**FEATURES:** Lakes, swimming, views, cliffs, flowers, waterfalls, wildlife, solitude

**DISTANCES:** Sifford Lakes 3.3 miles (5.3 km), Kings Creek Meadows 4.6 miles (7.3 km), Kings Creek Falls via Sifford Lake 6.1 miles (9.4 km), Corral Meadow 9.0 miles (14.6 km), Warner Valley Campground

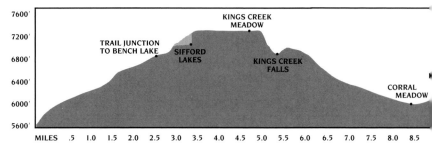

11.4 miles (18.5 km)

**TIME:** Allow 6 hours

**WILDLIFE:** Grouse, deer, eagle, quail

**HISTORY:** Kings Creek Meadows and Falls are named after James M. King, who lived in the meadows. He ran horses and mules in the area. He also operated a horse racing track in the Sacramento Valley at Pine Grove in the 1860's. His son, Oscar King, was born in a hemlock log cabin in the meadows.

---

The trail rises steeply, approximately 500 vertical feet, for 1.0 miles to the trail junction to Kings Creek forking to the left (west). The trail is well engineered and consequently not as difficult as it would seem. This first mile is part of the famous Pacific Crest Trail which extends from Canada to Mexico. The trail provides excellent views of Drakesbad, Red Mountain (renamed Sifford Mountain) and Warner Valley to the south. The trail continues from the trail junction gradually uphill. After approximately .7 of a mile there is an excellent view of Sifford Mountain and the trail going to Drake Lake on the right or west side of it. The trail slowly gains elevation, and the forest changes from predominately White to Red Fir. There are interesting examples of snow bend with some trees having three or more distinct bends. Lake Almanor can be seen 2.3 miles from the start.

There is a trail junction 2.6 miles from the start with Sifford lakes .7 of a mile and Kings Creek Meadows 2.0 miles straight ahead (west). To the right (north), Bench Lake is .4 of a mile and Kings Creek Falls 1.0 miles. Hikers at this point can choose to bypass Sifford Lakes and Kings Creek Meadows and hike directly to Kings Creek Falls. This would shorten the hike by approximately 1.6 miles. The trail to Bench Lake is level for .1 of a mile and then ascends the ridge fairly steeply for the next .3 of a mile. When returning to the main trail, you rise steeply for .3 of a mile to the junction to Sifford Lakes, which is .4 of a mile to the left (south). This portion of the hike to Sifford Lakes is described on page 27, "Kings Creek Meadows to Sifford Lakes." Five tenths of a mile further from the cut-off to Sifford Lakes, leave the main trail and hike north for a few hundred feet for a panoramic view of Mt. Harkness, Saddle and Pilot Mountains and Warner Valley. In another .7 of a mile, the trail crosses Kings Creek.

In a few hundred feet, the trail connects with the trail to Kings Creek Falls, .6 of a mile further to the right (east). The trail descends from the trail junction through a forest of predominately Lodgepole Pine, Mountain Hemlock and Red Fir. After .1 of a mile, the trail forks with the horse trail going to the left .8 of a mile and to the right .5 of a mile via the Cascade foot trail. Straight ahead is the Cascade View .1 of a mile, well worth the short hike and is an excellent place to photograph the Cascades. The foot trail down the edge of the Cascades is a "watch-your-step" one and if you have a fear of heights or a balance or agility problem, the horse trail might be a good choice. Two tenths of a mile from the falls, the horse trail rejoins the foot trail. A short distance past here, the trail to Bench lake (.6 of a mile) and Warner Valley (1.0 miles) forks to the right. The trail continues to descend

E

10.5    11.0

to the 50 foot falls. They should be photographed early in the day, prior to 1:00 pm, as there are shadows in the afternoon.

The trail to Corral Meadow swings north, to the left, away from the creek not the small foot path continuing downstream. After an initial steep climb of . of a mile, the trail starts a series of levels and descents. Approximately .3 of a mile after leaving the falls, the trail crosses an ice cold spring, an excellent spot for refilling your canteen. The trail continues descending through a series of springs and small meadows profuse in wildflowers including Queen Anne's Lac Large Leaf Lupine, Indian Paint Brush, Blue Penstemon, Pussy Paws, Cow Parsnip, Monkey Flower, Blue Monkshood, Corn Lily, Larkspur, Yarrow, Pennyroyal, Columbine, and Leopard Lily.

Two miles from the falls, the trail meets Kings Creek and crosses one of its tributaries coming from the left (west). Two tenths of a mile further, the trail joins the trail junction to Corral Meadow .7 of a mile, and Warner Valley is 3.1 miles to the right (south). Summit Lake is 1.7 miles to the left (north). One tent of a mile from the junction, the trail crosses Kings Creek and parallels it on its west side. Arriving at Corral Meadow there is a trail marker with Warner Valley 2.4 miles further. Corral Meadow is level with easy access to Kings Creek. There are a number of campsites here. It is a main trail junction with paths leading to Summit Lake 2.4 miles, Horseshoe Lake 4.5 miles, Lower Twin 4.6 miles, Cinder Cone 8.8 miles and Butte Lake 10.1 miles. Kelly Camp is 4.0 miles and Warner Valley Campground 2.4 miles. From Corral Meadow you rejoin the Pacific Crest Trail back to Drakesbad.

From Corral Meadow, the trail is mostly level for .2 of a mile where the trail to Kelly Camp branches to the left. From this point the trail climbs at a moderate to steep ascent for approximately .8 of a mile and finally levels for .2 of a mile before starting a gradual descent through a beautiful open forest of Western White and Jeffrey Pine. The trail rejoins the original trail junction to Kings Creek. The last mile of trail returns to the Warner Valley Campground.

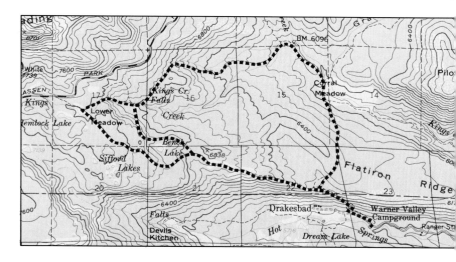

# 24 Drakesbad
*to Dream Lake*

| | |
|---|---|
| **TRAILHEAD:** | Parking lot west of Warner Valley Campground |
| **FEATURES:** | Lake |
| **DISTANCE:** | .7 of a mile (1.1 km) one way |
| **TIME:** | Allow one hour |
| **TOGRAPHY:** | Climbs 80 vertical feet |
| **WILDLIFE:** | Deer, marmot |
| **HISTORY:** | Refer to "History," see page 40 |

**AUTHOR'S COMMENTS:** Dream Lake is not mentioned on the trailhead sign. However, it is a short diversion from the trail to Devils Kitchen via Drakesbad Meadows. It can be used as an alternative to swimming in the Drakesbad Guest Ranch pool for those not staying at the Guest Ranch, or as a short hike to walk off dinner.

the trailhead, the sign reads Boiling Springs Lake .9 miles — 1.4 km; Devils tchen 2.1 miles — 3.4 km; Drake Lake 2.4 miles — 3.9 km; Terminal Geyser 2.7 iles — 4.3 km. At the start, the trail to Dream Lake is the same as the trail to evil's Kitchen, and as the self-guiding nature trail to Boiling Springs Lake. After of a mile, there is a junction with Devil's Kitchen 1.8 miles to the right. Boiling rings Lake is to the left .4 miles (.8 km), Drake Lake is 2.0 miles (3.3 km), Terminal Geyser is 2.3 miles (3.8 km). Proceeding to the right, the trail descends toard Hot Springs Creek and is joined by a path from Drakesbad Guest Ranch. e trail crosses a series of footbridges and swings westerly. After .2 of a mile om the previous trail junction, it comes to a trail marker sign reading Devils tchen 1.6 miles (2.6 km), Drake Lake 2.1 miles (3.4 km), Rice Creek 4.0 miles .5 km). Approximately 200 feet past the sign, there is a barely discernible footth branching to the left. The trail re-crosses Hot Springs Creek and ascends in southwesterly direction. The trail crosses the outlet creek and in .1 of a mile rives at the lake. A small mountain lake, it is not as spectacular as the name dicates, though on the right summer day, with the right person, it would be fun sit around. The lake is fed by a series of springs on the opposite side (south). n the return, note the interesting cliffs on the north side of Warner Valley. There e places with similar cliffs and rock formations extending all the way from fford Lakes to Lee Camp.

# 25 Drakesbad
*Devils Kitchen via Drake Lake, return to Warner Valley Campground via Drakesbad Guest Ranch*

| | |
|---|---|
| **TRAILHEAD:** | Parking lot west of Warner Valley Campground |

**FEATURES:** Forest, Meadow, hydrothermal activity

**DISTANCE:** Drake lake 2.4 miles (3.9 km), Devils Kitchen (via Drake Lake) 4.8 miles (7.8 km). Return to Warner Valley Campground (via Drakesbad Guest Ranch) 7.1 miles (11.5 km).

**TIME:** Allow 4 to 4½ hours

**HISTORY:** *Drake Lake*: Named after Edward R. Drake of Drakesbad who settled in the area in the 1860's.
*Devils Kitchen*: Name was probably given to the area by H. Brince, a photographer from Chico, California around 1879. It is aptly named for the natural boiling mud pots and fumaroles.

**AUTHOR'S COMMENTS:** I would recommend eliminating Drake Lake from the loop thus saving 2.0 miles of hard hiking if your time is limited, if you have small children, or you are not in reasonably good shape.

The first part of the hike is the same as to Terminal Geyser and Boiling Springs Lake. After approximately .1 of a mile, the trail crosses Hot Springs Creek. After .4 of a mile from the start, the trail to Devils Kitchen (not via Drake Lake) forks to the right (west) 1.8 miles. Fifty feet further, the trail again forks with the trail to Drake Lake 1.9 miles to the right (west). Approximately .2 of a mile from the fork, there is a huge White Fir on the right along with its two brothers which have gone to the happy hunting ground for White Fir. The trail mostly continues on a level in a westerly direction crossing a number of tributaries of Hot Springs Creek. The forest in this section has a great deal of slash and debris. Portions of the Park are in a natural fire zone where natural ignited fire will be monitored under prescribed conditions.

After 1.4 miles from the start, the trail forks with the trail to Devils Kitchen 1.4 miles to the right (north) and the other fork to Drake Lake 1.0 miles and Rice Creek is 2.9 miles. Two tenths of a mile further, the trail turns south and starts a fairly steep ascent rising approximately 640 feet in .8 of a mile (12.9% grade). It is open but for a few White Pine, so there is practically no shade. The lake is not deep enough to swim in dry years. There are millions of tiny red bugs in the water which also discourage drinking.

Leaving Drake Lake, you return 1.0 miles to the trail junction to Devils Kitchen 1.4 miles. A little over .1 of a mile from the junction, the trail descends and crosses Hot Springs Creek. One tenth of a mile further, there is a grove of Aspen with the evidence of beaver at work. The trail then levels and passes through a magnificent stand of White Fir over 200 years old. After .5 of a mile from the junction, the trail joins the one coming from Drakesbad with .9 of a mile further to Devils Kitchen, and Warner Valley Campground 1.4 miles to the right (east). Continuing, the trail passes a beautiful grove of Jeffrey Pine and Incense Cedar. After a moderate rise, the trail descends for .1 of a mile rather steeply into Devils Kitchen. This hydrothermal area is bigger than the Sulphur Works but smaller than Bumpass Hell. Containing 7 acres, it has well constructed paths and bridges, and hikers are again cautioned to stay on the trails. Devils Kitchen was named for the mud pots on a shelf running above Hot Springs Creek which runs right through Devils Kitchen. The cliffs near Sifford Lakes can be seen to the northwest. On the return, after .9 of a mile, the trail rejoins the

nction to Drake Lake with 1.4 miles to Warner Creek Campground. The trail is
vel and the forest is mainly White Fir. After approximately .2 of a mile, it enters
e Drakesbad Meadow. There is a trail marker in Drakesbad Meadow indicating
ake Lake 2.1 miles, Rice Creek 4.0 miles, and Devils Kitchen 1.6 miles. The
ountain to the east is Mt. Harkness. Marmots can be observed in this area. For
e next .3 of a mile, the trail continues through the meadow to a fork, the left
ing to Drakesbad Guest Ranch. By hiking the road back from the Guest Ranch
ward the Ranger Station for .4 of a mile, the trail completes the loop. The
ght-hand fork crosses Hot Springs Creek, parallels it on its south side and
joins the original trail at trail marker #9, thus completing the loop. It then
turns .4 of a mile to the original trailhead.

# Drakesbad

*Terminal Geyser Loop via Boiling Springs Lake and Little Willow Lake*

**TRAILHEAD:** Parking lot area west of Warner Valley Campground

**FEATURES:** Wildflowers, forest, hydrothermal activity, solitude

**DISTANCE:** Boiling Springs Lake .9 miles (1.4 km), Terminal Geyser 2.7 miles
(4.3 km) one way. Add 1.1 miles (1.6 km) each way for detouring to
Little Willow Lake

**TIME:** Allow 3 to 3½ hours

**WILDLIFE:** Deer (2 bucks), mountain quail

**HISTORY:** *Terminal Geyser:* It is not a geyser but rather a fumarole. Formerly
called "Steamboat Springs," the word terminal is of unknown origin. My guess would be that it was meant to be thermal and was
misspelled by a mapmaker. In 1978, it was drilled and capped by
Phillips Petroleum Company which was doing geothermal exploration. To prevent further exploration, the Park Service condemned
this piece of private land in 1980.
*Little Willow Lake:* The name 'Little' is to distinguish it from the
larger Willow Lake. Willow was applied to these lakes because of
the abundant growth of this scrubby tree in these localities.

**AUTHOR'S** This is one of the best hikes in Lassen, with two areas of hydrother-
**COMMENTS:** mal activity and a tranquil forest. I don't recommend the side trip
to Willow Lake (1.1 miles each way) unless you have an interest in
hiking the Pacific Crest Trail from its southern entry into Lassen

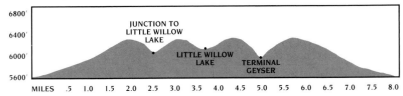

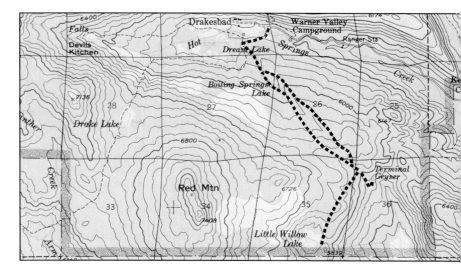

Park, or want to extend the hike to Terminal Geyser. Other reasons for hiking the side trip would be to see a lake well along in transition to a meadow. There is no water available on this hike.

At the trailhead, there are self-guiding nature leaflets available with numbered points of interest. For the first .1 of a mile, the trail is mainly level, paralleling Hot Springs Creek. At the point it crosses the creek, it starts to ascend gradually. There are wildflowers including Queen Anne's Lace, Monkey Flower, Aster, and Bull Thistle. After .4 miles the trail forks with the right going to Devils Kitchen 1.8 miles, and the left going to Boiling Springs Lake, Drake Lake and Terminal Geyser. Fifty feet further the trail forks again, the right going to Drake Lake (1.9 miles) and the left continuing to Boiling Springs Lake and Terminal Geyser. Ground cover is sparse and the forest consists of Lodgepole Pine, Incense Cedar, White and Red Fir (commonly known as Silvertip). There is another fork in the trail .7 of a mile from the start at guide marker #16 with the left going to Terminal Geyser (2.0 miles) and the right to the Boiling Springs Lake circuit. The route goes right and will return here after completing the loop. Two tenths of a mile further is Boiling Springs Lake. The self-guiding nature trail continues around the right side of the lake and the trail again forks at self-guiding marker #33 with Terminal Geyser 1.5 miles to the right (south). From this junction, the trail to Terminal Geyser climbs steeply and then has a series of moderate rises. The forest has some magnificent Cedar and Jeffrey Pine.

Two tenths of a mile before Terminal Geyser, the trail to Little Willow Lake forks to the right 1.1 miles. Little Willow is the southern point of the Pacific Crest Trail in Lassen Park. This junction is also where the loop joins from the trail mentioned .7 of a mile from the start. The trail to Little Willow Lake is marked with gray diagonal markers as well as the Pacific Crest Trail markers, instead of the normal yellow discs. After approximately .2 of a mile, the forest opens and Mt. Harkness is in view to the left (west). The trail has a series of undulations, ascending approximately 240 vertical feet, then descends steeply approximately .3 of a mile 240 vertical feet.

Hiking Trails of Lasser

Little Willow Lake is a good example of the transition that all Lassen lakes are gradually making: from lake to mountain meadow. It is more like a wet marsh than a lake. Though green and pretty, it offers no fishing or swimming. There is a Pacific Crest Trail register at the lake. Return to the original junction with Terminal Geyser .2 of a mile further. One tenth of a mile or so from Terminal Geyser, you can hear what sounds like cars on a freeway — don't be alarmed, it's Terminal Geyser. At this point, the trail descends steeply to the geyser. The turn-off is marked by a Park Service sign, but is easy to miss. If you come to a road you missed it, but just hike left for .1 of a mile on the road and you come to the geyser. The geyser is spectacular, emitting a good quantity of steam.

On the return, .2 of a mile from the Geyser, the trail forks and proceeds to the right to complete the loop to Warner Valley Campground, 2.5 miles (see map). For the next .6 of a mile, the trail gradually climbs through a beautiful open meadow. Lake Almanor can be plainly seen to the southeast. The trail then levels and re-enters the forest. Another .4 of a mile or so, you can leave the trail to the right for a short distance for a good view of Warner Valley, including Mt. Harkness, Saddle and Pilot Mountain. Due to the proximity of Drakesbad Guest Ranch, you may meet horseback riders, and they have the "right of way." Shortly, the trail starts a gradual to moderate descent. Many of the large older Cedar trees are badly charred at the base indicating a forest fire many hundreds of years ago. This section of forest is one of the best in the park. It is very peaceful and tranquil. I did not see another person on the entire hike, which was made in the middle of August. The trail returns to Boiling Springs Lake at nature trail marker #36. You can complete the nature trail, or continue on the trail directly back to the trailhead. The trail rejoins the Cold Boiling Lake trail at nature trail marker #16, thus completing the loop.

# 27 Juniper Lake

*Juniper Lake Ranger Station to Lower Twin Lake via Cameron Meadow and Horseshoe Lake, return via Grassy Swale*

**TRAILHEAD:** Juniper Lake Ranger Station

**FEATURES:** Lakes, meadows, streams

**DISTANCE:** Cameron Meadow 1.6 miles (2.7 km), Horseshoe Lake 3.7 miles (6.0 km), Lower Twin Lake 7.6 miles (12.3 km), return Juniper Lake Ranger Station 14.0 miles (22.7 km).

**TIME:** Allow 7 to 7 ½ hours

**WILDLIFE:** Deer

**HISTORY:** *Cameron Meadow*: Named for Jeff Cameron who had a homestead there and leased the surrounding country for cattle grazing. The remains of an old cabin are still in evidence.
*Lower and Upper Twin Lakes*: see page 36.
*Horseshoe Lake*: see page 61.
*Grassy Swale*: see page 38.

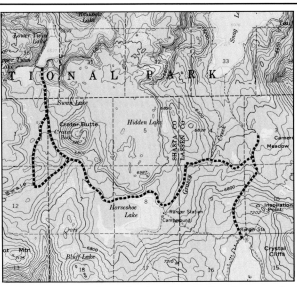

At the trailhead, the sign reads: *to the right Cameron Meadow 1.6 miles (2.7 km), Jakey Lake 2.8 miles (4.5 km), Snag Lake 2.9 miles (4.6 km), Butte Lake 7.1 miles (11.5 km), Cinder Cone 7.6 miles (12.2 km). To the left Horseshoe Lake 1.4 miles (2.2 km), Lower Twin Lake 5.3 miles (8.5 km), Corral Meadow 6.7 miles (10.7 km), Summit Lake 9.0 miles (14.5 km), Warner Valley 9.1 miles (14.6 km).* Initially, the trail is the same as to Jakey Lake, described on page 56. For the first .4 of a mile, the trail ascends moderately, then levels. For the next .2 of a mile, the trail is level and then for the next .6 of a mile, starts a sharp descent of some 500 vertical feet. The trail levels, and .1 of a mile further, the trail forks, with the right trail going to Jakey Lake 1.5 miles (2.5 km), Widow Lake 7.5 miles (12.0 km), to the left Snag Lake 1.6 miles (2.6 km). From the trail junction, the trail descends crossing a stream with many wildflowers. Three tenths of a mile further, there is another trail junction with the trail to Horseshoe Lake 2.1 miles (3.4 km) to the left (west), Snag Lake 1.3 miles (2.1 km). To see Cameron Meadow, you must proceed .1 of a mile further toward Snag Lake to the remains of the Cameron Homestead Cabin and then backtrack to the trail junction. From the trail junction, the trail goes west and crosses a small stream. After another .3 of a mile, it passes by a beautiful meadow on the right (north). The trail is mostly level. The trail is well-marked with red and yellow discs. After 1.2 miles from the previous trail junction, the trail crosses Grassy Creek and immediately joins the Snag Lake, Horseshoe Lake trail with Horseshoe Lake to the left (south) .9 of a mile (1.4 km), Snag Lake to the right (north) 1.4 miles (2.2 km) and Jakey Lake back 3.0 miles (4.8 km). The trail parallels the west side of Grassy Creek in a southerly direction. This section of the trail is considered to be one of the nicest in the Park.

After .9 of a mile, there is a trail junction with Snag Lake 2.3 miles (3.5 km), Cinder Cone 6.6 miles (10.6 km), Butte Lake 6.9 miles (11.1 km) back (north)

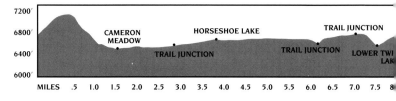

the right (west) Lower Twin Lake 3.9 miles (6.2 km), Corral Meadow 5.2 miles
.4 km), Warner Valley 7.7 miles (12.4 km). To the left (east) Juniper Lake is 1.4
iles (2.3 km), Indian Lake 1.5 miles (2.5 km). From the trail junction, the Hor-
·shoe Lake Ranger Station is visible on the other side of Grassy Creek, and
issen Peak is visible to the west. The level trail swings to the northwest and
ɔes around the north side of Horseshoe Lake. After .8 of a mile, it leaves the
ke, ascends briefly, and levels through a forest of Lodgepole Pine. It passes by
veral small lakelets, and Crater Butte is in the forefront. The trail follows the
eek and descends to a junction with Warner Valley 5.5 miles (8.9 km), Corral
eadow 3.1 miles (5.0 km) to the left front, to the right (north) Lower Twin Lake is
7 miles (2.8 km), Cinder Cone 5.9 miles (9.5 km), Butte Lake 7.2 miles (11.6 km).
ıck is Horseshoe Lake 1.4 miles (2.2 km), and Juniper Lake 3.6 miles (5.7 km).

    After .8 of a mile from the previous trail junction, there is another junc-
ɔn joining the Pacific Crest Trail with Lower Twin Lake .9 of a mile (1.5 km)
raight ahéad, Horseshoe Lake back 2.2 miles (3.5 km), Corral Meadow to the
ft 3.7 miles (5.9 km), Warner Valley 6.1 miles (9.8 km). Three tenths of a mile
ırther, Swan Lake appears to the right. The trail junctions at Lower Twin Lake
th Upper Twin Lake .5 of a mile, and Summit Lake 4.1 miles to the left (west).
> the right (along the Pacific Crest Trail) Snag Lake is 3.0 miles, Cinder Cone 4.2
iles, Badger Flat 5.4 miles, and Butte Lake 5.5 miles. From Lower Twin Lake the
ıil goes back .9 of a mile (1.5 km) to the previous trail junction. From here, the
ıil takes a right (west) fork to Corral Meadow 3.7 miles (5.9 km).

    After .4 of a mile from the junction, the trail starts a moderate to steep
·scent, following the stream until the headwaters of Grassy Swale Creek. The
ıil swings right (west) for .3 of a mile to the trail junction with Corral Meadow
4 miles (3.9 km), Warner Valley 4.8 miles (7.8 km)
ı the right fork, and Horseshoe Lake 2.0 miles (3.3
า) to the left, and back Lower Twin Lake 2.2 miles
5 km), Cinder Cone 6.4 miles (10.3 km), Butte Lake
7 miles (12.4 km). Another hike is to continue
uth. When the trail descends into Grassy Swale
eek, pick up the trail on the other side (south side)
the creek, thus shortening the hike .6 of a mile.
ɔm the trail junction, the trail goes south across
ʌassy Swale Creek leaving the Pacific Crest Trail,
d then turns left (east) on the other side of the
ʒek. The trail climbs gradually, then steepens for .7
a mile back to the trail junction branching to
wer Twin Lake to the north. The trail returns to

ɔrseshoe Lake 1.4 miles with another .9 of a mile to the Horseshoe Ranger
ıtion. From here, it is 1.3 miles to the Juniper Lake Ranger Station as de-
ribed in "Juniper Lake Ranger Station to Snag Lake, return via Horseshoe
Lake," page 54.

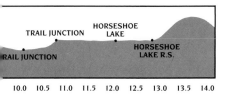

# 28 Juniper Lake

*Juniper Lake Campground to Mt. Harkness, return on its west side and south side of Juniper Lake*

**TRAILHEAD:** Juniper Lake Campground

**FEATURES:** Wildflowers, scenic views, wildlife

**DISTANCE:** 1.9 miles (3.1 km) to Mt. Harkness, 5.5 miles (8.9 km) for Mt. Harkness-Juniper Lake loop.

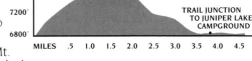

**TIME:** 3 to 3½ hours, 2½ hours to return directly on same route

**WILDLIFE:** Many deer, mountain quail, grouse

**HISTORY:** Named in honor of Harvey W. Harkness, president of the California Academy of Sciences in San Francisco from 1887 to 1895.

**AUTHOR'S COMMENTS:** No power boats are allowed on Juniper Lake. The only drinking water available is boiled lake water.

The trail ascends gradually for .1 of a mile through a forest of Lodgepole Pine and Red Fir, then it steepens with a series of switchbacks. Glimpses of Juniper Lake are to the right. Ground cover is Pinemat Manzanita with some wildflowers including Blue Penstemon and Silver Leaf Lupine. As the trail gains elevation, the Lodgepole Pine gives way to Western White Pine. After a 1.2 mile climb of approximately 600 feet, the slopes become open with a few scattered trees. Lava flows are visible on top of the ridge to the right, and there is an outcropping straight ahead. The trail swings to the right and re-enters the forest. Mountain Hemlock are abundant. Deer are quite common, however, the herd is migratory and their habitat is at a lower elevation in early spring and late fall. Wildflowers include Pennyroyal and in August, the Yellow Bloomers Golden Bush is in bloom along with Silver Leaf Lupine. After another .2 of a mile, there is a grand view of Lassen Peak to the west. At the junction for the trail return via the south shore of Juniper Lake, there is a view of two lonely Western White Pine with their tops bent to attest to the direction from which the storms come. Another switchback in the trail brings us to the Mt. Harkness Lookout. A fabulous view awaits: To the east beyond Susanville, to the south Lake Almanor, and the northern Sierra Nevada. To the north Mt. Shasta, Cinder Cone, Juniper Lake, Mt. Hoffman, Fairfield Peak, Red Cinder Cone and Red Cinder. To the west Drakesbad, Lassen Peak, Brokeoff, Diller. In fact, most of the Park is in view.

Returning to the junction, the trail splits left for the return loop via the south side of Juniper Lake. The forest is Mountain Hemlock and Red Fir with ground cover of Silverleaf Lupine or Pinemat Manzanita and Pennyroyal. The rocky trail descends steeply and caution is advised. The forest is fairly open with good views of interesting rock slides and formations with Lassen Peak to the refront. After 1.7 miles, there is a trail junction. To the right (north) Juniper ake Ranger Station 2.8 miles, Indian Lake 1.8 miles, Horseshoe Lake 2.6 miles, the left Warner Valley Road 2.4 miles. To the right rear (northeast) Juniper ake Campground 1.8 miles. The trail from this point is level. After a short distance, the trail joins the south side of Juniper Lake. The shore is rocky and approaches for swimming aren't good. The best swimming is on a beach near the anger Station on the north side of the lake. Watch for the mountain quail that habit this area. After 1.8 miles, the trail enters the west side of the Juniper ake Campground.

# 29 Juniper Lake

*Juniper Lake Road to Crystal Lake*

**TRAILHEAD:** Three tenths of a mile north of the campground towards the Ranger Station

7600'  
7200'  
6800'  

CRYS-TAL LK.

MI. .4

**FEATURES:** Scenery, lake, forest, fishing

**DISTANCE:** Four tenths of a mile (.7 km) and return for a total of .8 of a mile (1.3 km).

**TIME:** Allow 1/2 hour for hiking plus time spent at the lake

**HISTORY:** *Crystal Lake*: So called because of the crystal clarity of its water.

**AUTHOR'S COMMENTS:** This is an excellent trail, and good for children. It's a good hike to take a picnic lunch because of the lake's beauty, you feel like you want to stay for awhile. Take extra film for your camera. The crystal clear water cleanses the mind and body as well as the soul.

he trail ascends steeply through a orest of Red and White Fir and Western White Pine. Ground cover is sparse vith Manzanitas, Pinemat and Green eaf. The last .2 of a mile are open, revealing grand views of Juniper Lake to the vest, Mt. Harkness to the south, and Lassen Peak to the northwest. The reward t the crest of the trail is a view of Crystal Lake, considered by many to be assen Park's most beautiful. The lake is appropriately named and appears as a himmering jewel. A hike around the lake is a must. Beautiful views in all lirections combined with varying and interesting rock formations are a photographer's dream. There are fish in the lake. The water is colder than most of the other lakes in the Park, nevertheless swimming is enjoyably refreshing. Hike a short distance above the rocks on the south side of the lake and there are fabulous views of Juniper and Crystal Lakes, Lake Almanor and Lassen Peak.

# 30 Juniper Lake
*Juniper Lake Ranger Station to Snag Lake, return via Horseshoe Lake*

**TRAILHEAD:** Juniper Lake Ranger Station

**FEATURES:** Forest, lakes, wildflowers, mountain meadows and stream.

**DISTANCE:** Cameron Meadow 1.6 miles (2.7 km), Snag Lake 2.9 miles (4.7 km), Horseshoe Lake 5.5 miles (8.9 km), Juniper Lake Ranger Station 6.9 miles (11.2 km).

**TIME:** Allow 4½ hours

**WILDLIFE:** Grouse, deer, geese, ducks

**HISTORY:** *Snag Lake*: Formed by lava flows from Cinder Cone damming Grassy Creek and drowning the trees which became snags. The snags have fallen through the years until few remain visible.

**AUTHOR'S COMMENTS:** This hike has two-fold enjoyment. On some hikes, such as Crystal Lake, the hike isn't so much, it's the destination that is the important feature. In this hike, both the destinations of Snag and Horseshoe Lakes are worthwhile, and the hike itself is outstanding.

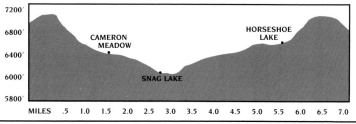

On the outset the trail is the same as the one to Jakey Lake, described on page 56. For the first .4 of a mile, the trail ascends then levels. The forest of Red Fir, Western White and Lodgepole Pine is rather open as the trail proceeds in a northerly direction. The forest floor is mostly Pinemat Manzanita. For the next .2 of a mile, the trail is level and then for the next .6 of a mile, starts a sharp decline of some 500 vertical feet. The trail levels, and .1 of a mile further, the trail forks with the right trail going to Jakey Lake 1.5 miles (2.5 km), Widow Lake 7.5 miles (12.0 km); to the left Snag Lake 1.6 miles (2.6 km). From the junction, the trail descends crossing a stream with many wildflowers. Three tenths of a mile further, there is another trail junction with the trail to Horseshoe Lake 2.1 miles (3.4 km) to the left (west), Snag Lake 1.3 miles (2.1 km) straight ahead (north), and Jakey Lake 1.8 miles (2.9 km) back. The trail passes through a number of small meadows with wildflowers including Pussy Paws, Columbine, Senecio,

54                                                          Hiking Trails of Lassen

Aster, Lupine, and Corn Lily. Another .1 of a mile further, the trail passes the remains of an old settler's cabin off to the right. Cameron Meadow is to the right (east) with a view of Mt. Hoffman. The trail crosses additional springs flowing into and out of the meadow.

Leaving the Cameron Meadow, the trail passes several small meadows of wildflowers, Sky Rocket Gilia, Bull Thistle and yellow wildflowers. The trail descends into the Snag Lake trail junction. To the left Horseshoe Lake is 2.6 miles, Lower Twin Lake 3.7 miles, Cinder Cone 4.7 miles. To the right Butte Lake is 4.3 miles, to the rear Juniper Lake 2.9 miles, and Jakey Lake 3.1 miles. At the trail junction, Snag Lake is not in view. To reach Snag Lake, proceed to the right (east) in the direction to Butte Lake for .2 of a mile where the trail swings near the lake, with views of Cinder Cone to the north and the Fantastic Lava Beds to the south. Canadian honkers can be observed.

Back at the previously described trail junction to Horseshoe lake, the trail travels level in a westerly direction. It crosses several small springs flowing into the lake, providing water for nice campsites along the south shore. One tenth of a mile past the trail junction, a footbridge crosses Grassy Creek, and the forest opens and is much drier, but continues to be mainly Lodgepole Pine. The trail forks .3 of a mile further. To the right is Butte Lake Ranger Station via Cinder Cone 5.7 miles, Rainbow Lake 2.5 miles, Lower Twin Lake 3.3 miles. To the left Horseshoe Lake is 2.2 miles, Juniper Lake via Horseshoe Lake 3.7 miles, Juniper Lake via Cameron Meadow 3.2 miles back. From the junction, the trail climbs gradually through a moderately dense forest of White and Red Fir and Lodgepole and Western White Pine. The ground cover is Pinemat Manzanita and wildflowers. Six tenths of a mile from the trail junction, the trail proceeds up the west edge of Grassy Creek. Further .5 of a mile, the trail switches back and forth over the creek. In .2 of a mile, there is a trail junction, to the left (east) Cameron Meadow 1.2 miles (1.9 km), Jakey Lake 3.0 miles (4.8 km), straight ahead is Horseshoe Lake .9 of a mile (1.4 km), Snag Lake 1.4 miles (2.2 km) to the rear. As the trail continues, it passes a series of meadows on the left — hence the name Grassy Creek.

At the trail junction, the trail intersects the Juniper Lake trail with Juniper Lake 1.4 miles (2.3 km), Indian Lake 1.5 miles (2.5 km) left (east), straight ahead Lower Twin Lake 3.9 miles (6.2 km), Corral Meadow 5.2 miles (8.4 km), Warner

Valley 7.7 miles (12.4 km). In order to reach the shore of Horseshoe Lake, proceed straight ahead on the Twin Lake route for .1 of a mile. There will be found one of the classic views of Lassen Park to the west. To the south are views of Pilot and Saddle Mountains. There is a sandy beach with good swimming. Backtracking to the trail fork to Juniper Lake, the trail crosses Grassy Creek. The Ranger Station is here. It is manned from mid-June through mid-October depending on weather and snow. In case of emergencies, they can radio out. One tenth of a mile past the junction, the trail forks to the right (south) to the campground and Indian Lake 1.4 miles (2.2 km), west to Snag Lake 2.4 miles (3.8 km), Cinder Cone 6.7 miles (10.8 km), Butte Lake 7.0 miles (11.3 km), Lower Twin Lake 4.0 miles (6.5 km), Corral Meadow 5.4 miles (8.6 km), and Warner Valley 7.8 miles (12.6 km). Juniper Lake is east 1.3 miles (2.1 km). The trail follows an old road through a forest of Red Fir, Western White and Lodgepole Pine in an easterly direction. The trail climbs steeply approximately 400 vertical feet in the next .5 of a mile. The trail levels and starts a gradual to moderate descent to the Ranger Station.

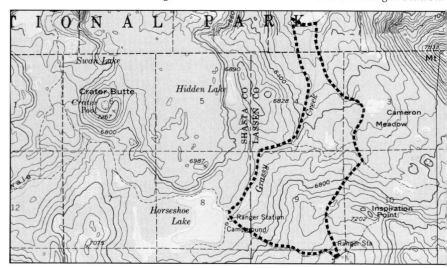

# 31 Juniper Lake

*To Butte Lake via Jakey Lake, Red Cinder Cone and Widow Lake*

**TRAILHEAD:** Juniper Lake Ranger Station

**FEATURES:** Wildlife, ducks, deer, lakes

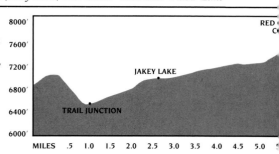

Hiking Trails of Lassen

**DISTANCE:** Jakey Lake 2.8 miles (4.5 km), Red Cinder Cone approximately 5.8 miles (9.5 km), Widow Lake 8.8 miles (14.3 km), Butte Lake Campground 12.4 miles (20.1 km) one way.

**TIME:** Allow 8 hours (allow for overnight camping)

**HISTORY:** *Jakey Lake*: Named for Jakey Olson, who had a homestead there. The Olsons were pioneers with the Kelly family of Warner Valley. *Red Cinder and Red Cinder Cone*: The names are purely descriptive.

**AUTHOR'S COMMENTS:** There is no water available. This hike, because of its length, is best done backpacking or camping overnight at Butte Lake with a return via Cinder Cone and Snag Lake. It's best to refill at Grassy Creek.

or the first .4 of a mile, the trail has a gradual ascent through a moderately pen forest of Red Fir, Western White and Lodgepole Pine. It levels and contin-es in a northerly direction. After .2 of a mile, the trail starts a series of descents, arying from steep to gentle, and the forest becomes dense. Ground cover is Pine-hat Manzanita with some wildflowers. The trail levels, and after 1.3 miles from he start, there is a trail junction with Jakey Lake to the right 1.5 miles (2.5 km), Vidow Lake 7.5 miles (12.0 km); to the left Snag Lake 1.6 miles (2.7 km). The trail tarts a gradual rise paralleling an intermittent stream which is Jakey Lake Creek owing out of Jakey Lake. Along the bank are numerous wildflowers. Five tenths f a mile from the trail junction, there is a swampy area on the right were ducks an be observed and Inspiration Point is visible. Three tenths of a mile further, here is a huge White Pine with two trunks measuring approximately 26 feet in ircumference at breast height. From here, the trail ascends gradually to moder-tely for .3 of a mile, when it levels. After another .4 of a mile, the trail arrives at akey Lake. The trail sign indicates Snag Lake is 3.1 miles (5.0 km) to the rear, nd Widow Lake 6.0 miles (9.6 km) straight ahead. The trail proceeds along the outh edge of Jakey Lake. Wildflowers include Buttercups, Corn Lily and Aster. ampsites are just off the trail. About half way around Jakey Lake is a good spot for wimming. The bottom is a little muddy, but the water is pleasant in late summer.

The trail continues ascending past an inlet to the lake. It passes a num-er of small lakes on the right. Seven tenths of a mile past the lake, the trail wings left in a northerly direction. It passes a rather ugly lake on the left — akes are like people, they have varying degrees of beauty. One mile from Jakey ake, there is a very snaggy lake on the right. The trail ascends gradually and hen becomes steep. Climbing approximately 250 feet in .3 of a mile, the trail evels as it passes through the saddle between Red Cinder Cone and Red Cinder. The trail skirts a number of lava flows on the left. The forest of Red Fir with Western White Pine is open with Pinemat Manzanita as ground cover.

0   7.5   8.0   8.5   9.0   9.5   10.0   10.5   11.0   11.5   12.0   12.5   13.0

The trail descends gradually with a series of undulations for 2.5 miles to Widow Lake, passing a little dried up pond on the right and a sma lakelet on the left. Widow Lake is larger than Jakey Lake and a little lower in elevation. This lake has fewe mosquitoes than Jakey Lake and the water temperature is similar. There ar campsites, it is easy to walk round, and there is excellent swimming in A gust and early September. The trail goes around the west side for .1 of a mile, then descends steeply for .5 of a mile following a talus slope on the right. For the next .5 of a mile, you continue at a moderate descent through a fern meadow and follow an intermittent stream on the right. The trail switches across this stream several times, levels, and .4 of a mile further joins a trail junction with Butte Lake Ranger Station 2.4 miles further. One tenth of a mile past the trail sign marker, the trail enters a grove of Asp with Butte Lake visible through the trees. The trail continues level following the east shore through a Ponderosa for est. From the northeast corner of the lake, the trail rises steeply for .2 of a mile (seems like more) and then descends .7 of a mile to the Ranger Station.

# 32 Juniper Lake

*Juniper Lake Ranger Station to Inspiration Point*

**TRAILHEAD:** One tenth of a mile east of the Juniper Lake Ranger Station

**FEATURES:** Forest and scenic views

**DISTANCE:** Six tenths of a mile (1.0 km) and return

7200'
6800'
MILES .5 1.0

**TIME:** Allow 1 hour

**HISTORY:** Named by C. P. Snell, owner of the former Juniper Lake resort, for its truly inspirational view.

**AUTHOR'S COMMENTS:** The view from Inspiration Point, though not as spectacular as the view from Mt. Harkness, is inspirational, and would be a good sub stitute for hikers who have small children or are unable to climb 1,300 vertical feet required for Mt. Harkness. Another suggestion i

58

Hiking Trails of Lasse

to combine the hike to Jakey or Snag Lake by hiking west or northwest from Inspiration Point until you intersect the Juniper Lake-Snag Lake trail running north and south.

The beginning of the trail rises gradually through a moderately open, pretty forest of Red Fir and Lodgepole Pine. After .1 of a mile, the trail steepens to a moderate to steep ascent, and with the exception of .1 of a mile where it levels, it continues that way to the top. Western White and Jeffrey Pine join the forest as the elevation increases. From Inspiration Point, Prospect Peak, Cinder Cone and Snag Lake are clearly visible to the north. Mt. Shasta and Butte Lake are barely visible. Lassen Peak, Chaos Crags, the whole cauldron panorama of Diller and Brokeoff are to the west. Mt. Harkness and Juniper Lake are visible to the south, as well as Saddle Mountain to the southwest. To the northeast is Mt. Hoffman and Red Cinder Cone. Inpsiration Point is actually more of a ridge running east and west and it's worthwhile taking a few minutes to travel across the ridge to the west. For picture taking, the hike is best in the morning with the sun facing the most prominent features to the north and west. Wildflowers blooming in August are mostly Bloomer's Golden Bush. Return via the same way.

# 33 Juniper Lake

*Hike around Juniper Lake*

**TRAILHEAD:** Anywhere around the lake

**FEATURES:** Lake, swimming

**DISTANCE:** 6.4 miles (10.4 km) (3.1 miles (5.0 km) road, 3.3 miles (5.4 km) trail)

**TIME:** 3½ to 4 hours

**WILDLIFE:** Grouse, quail, deer, ducks

**TOPOGRAPHY:** Mostly level

**HISTORY:** Juniper Lake was named after the Juniper trees on the east slope overlooking the lake in the vicinity of Crystal Lake and Crystal Cliffs. The Juniper tree is quite rare in Lassen Park. The lake has also been called "Louisa" by some in the past.

Starting at the Juniper Lake Ranger Station and proceeding south along the west shore, the trail is a private road. The trail passes private homes through a predominately Red Fir forest. Crystal Cliffs are in view to the east. It has its ups and downs, and after 1.2 miles, the road stops at a chained gate at a private cabin. Continuing south, the trail is marked with yellow discs nailed to a tree. White Fir makes an appearance, and after .4 of a mile from the road ending, there is a bay in the lake with a place to swim. In another .6 of a mile, the trail swings away from the lake and descends steeply for .1 of a mile to a trail junction with Juniper Lake Ranger Station back 2.3 miles (3.7 km), to the right Indian Lake 1.3 miles (2.1 km), Horseshoe Lake 2.2 miles (3.5 km), to the left Mt. Harkness 2.1 miles

(3.4 km), Juniper Lake Campground 2.2 miles (3.5 km) and Warner Valley Road 2.8 miles (4.5 km). From here, the trail swings away from the lake to the south for .4 of a mile to another trail junction with Juniper Lake Campground to the left rear (northeast) 1.8 miles (2.8 km), Warner Valley to the right (west) 2.4 miles (3.8 km), Mount Harkness Lookout straight ahead 1.7 miles (2.7 km). To the rear, Juniper Lake Ranger Station is 2.8 miles (4.5 km), Indian Lake 1.8 miles (2.8 km), Horseshoe Lake 2.6 miles (4.3 km). The

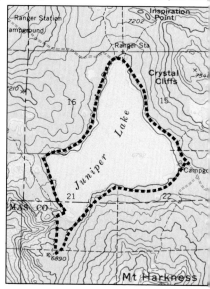

trail from this point is level. After a short distance, the trail joins the south side of Juniper Lake. The shore is rocky and approaches for swimming aren't good. The best swimming is on a beach near the Ranger Station on the north side of the lake. After 1.8 miles, the trail enters the west side of the Juniper Lake Campground. From the Juniper Lake Campground, the trail is the road for .4 of a mile to the main road to the Juniper Lake Ranger Station from Chester. Turning left (north), the road goes for .3 of a mile to the trailhead to Crystal Lake and continues more or less level for 1.2 miles further to the Ranger Station.

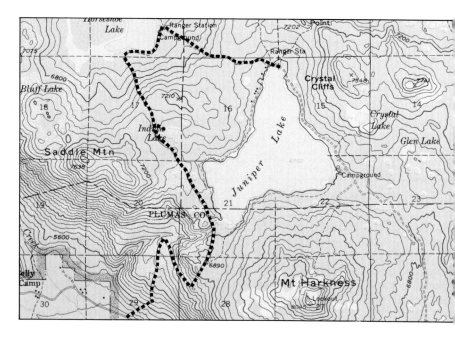

Hiking Trails of Lasse

# 34 Juniper Lake

*Juniper Lake Ranger Station to Warner Valley Road via Horseshoe and Indian Lakes*

**TRAILHEAD:** Juniper Lake Ranger Station

**FEATURES:** Lakes, forest, views

**DISTANCE:** Horseshoe Lake 1.4 miles (2.3 km), Indian Lake 2.8 miles (4.5 km), Warner Valley Road 6.9 miles (11.2 km)

**TIME:** 3 to 3½ hours

**HISTORY:** *Indian Lake:* History unknown. The Indians who frequented the area were the Atsugewi (Hat Creek Indians).
*Horseshoe Lake:* Originally called "Grassy Lake" because of its grassy edge. Renamed "Horseshoe Lake" because of its horseshoe shape.

**AUTHOR'S COMMENTS:** There is no water available except the lake — boil before drinking. The hike from the trail junction to Mt. Harkness down to Warner Valley is like finding a hidden jewel. It should be hiked in the direction I've described because it is downhill and you're facing all the majestic views to the west. Either ferry a vehicle to the trailhead in Warner Valley or arrange transportation to pick you up. The trailhead in Warner Valley is .7 of a mile past Lee Camp towards Drakesbad, or .8 of a mile from where the pavement ends back towards Chester, or 2.6 miles from the Drakesbad Ranger Station.

The trail ascends at a gradual to moderate rate through a forest of Red Fir with some Lodgepole Pine for .3 of a mile. The trail then levels for .1 of a mile, and then descends 1.0 mile for the rest of the way to the trail junction to Indian Lake located on the east shore of Juniper Lake. Indian Lake is 1.4 miles (2.2 km) to the left (south), to the right the Ranger Station at Snag Lake 2.4 miles (3.8 km), Cinder Cone 6.7 miles (10.8 km), Butte Lake 7.0 miles (11.3 km), Lower Twin Lake 4.0 miles (6.5 km), Corral Meadow 5.4 miles (8.6 km), and Warner Valley Campground 7.8 miles (12.6 km). The trail proceeds in a southerly direction through a forest of Red Fir and Lodgepole Pine. After .3 of a mile, it starts a steep climb of approximately 500 vertical feet. One tenth of a mile from the top, the forest opens with spectacular views of Lassen Peak and Chaos Crags to the west, Hat Mountain to the northwest, East and West Prospect Peaks to the north, and Brokeoff is barely visible to the southwest.

The trail follows the ridge top in a southeasterly direction, and is mostly level for .4 of a mile to the Indian Lake trail sign. Crystal Cliffs are visible to the east and Mt. Harkness to the forefront. The trail descends from the main trail steeply .1 of a mile to the lake at elevation 6,972 feet. The trail enters the lake on its west shore. It has a grassy perimeter and is a typical mountain lake. The bottom looked a little on the muddy side for swimming. Returning to the main trail, it continues mostly level with the exception of a few undulations. It passes between several lakelets, and .7 of a mile from the Indian Lake sign starts a descent to a trail junction sign indicating Indian Lake 1.3 miles (2.1 km), Horseshoe Lake 2.2 miles (3.5 km) back, Juniper Lake Ranger Station left (north) 2.3 miles (3.7 km) and straight ahead (south) Mt. Harkness 2.1 miles (3.4 km), Juniper Lake Campground 2.2 miles (3.5 km), and Warner Valley Road 2.8 miles (4.5 km). Four tenths of a mile further, there is another trail junction with Juniper Lake Campground to the left-rear (northeast) 1.8 miles (2.8 km), Warner Valley to the right (west) 2.4 miles (3.8 km), Mount Harkness Lookout straight ahead 1.7 miles (2.7 km). To the rear Juniper Lake Ranger Station 2.8 miles (4.5 km), Indian Lake 1.8 miles (2.8 km), Horseshoe Lake 2.6 miles (4.3 km).

    The trail heads west for .2 of a mile and then starts a steep descent. There are beautiful views of Lassen Peak to the west. Kelly Mountain is to the forefront. Drakesbad Meadow is visible and there are interesting rock formations to the right-rear. Terminal Geyser can be seen doing its thing. It's a well engineered trail similar to the one out of Drakesbad up to Flatiron Ridge. As the trail descends, it enters a beautiful stand of Incense Cedar. Their blackened trunks indicate a fire in the past. The trail continues its steep descent to the trailhead on the Warner Valley Road, the sign indicating Mt. Harkness Lookout back 4.0 miles (6.5 km), Juniper Lake Campground 4.1 miles (6.6 km), Indian Lake 4.1 miles (6.6 km), Horseshoe Lake 5.0 miles (8.0 km).

# 35 Butte Lake

*Butte Lake to Lower Twin Lake via Cinder Cone and Nobles Emigrant Trail, return via Rainbow Lake*

**TRAILHEAD:** Butte Lake Ranger Station

**FEATURES:** Emigrant Trail, lakes, swimming, volcanic phenomena

**DISTANCE:** From Ranger Station, Lower Twin Lake 6.9 miles (11.2 km), Rainbow Lake 7.5 miles (12.0 km), Cinder Cone 10.8 miles (17.5 km), return to Butte Lake Ranger Station 12.3 miles (19.8 km)

**TIME:** 6½ hours

**HISTORY:** Cinder Cone, see page 68, Lower Twin Lake, see page 36, Butte Lake see page 69.
*Nobles Emigrant Trail* is named after William H. Noble who blazed the trail and collected $2,000.00 from Redding, CA, merchants for disclosing "a route for a wagon road which would be superior in every respect to routes previously traveled."
*Rainbow Lake* was possibly named for the rainbow trout that used to be planted.

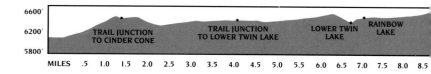

e initial part of the
 route is the self-guiding
nature trail to Cinder
Cone (see page 83). It is
also the Nobles Emi-
grant Trail. From the na-
ture guide marker #3,
Cinder Cone is 1.2 miles
(2.0 km), Lower Twin
Lake 4.9 miles (7.8 km),
Horseshoe Lake 7.5
miles (12.2 km), Juniper
Lake 8.5 miles (13.8 km),
Summit Lake 9.2 miles
(14.8 km), Hat Lake 12.3
miles (19.8 km). Along
the trail, there are dead
snags still standing with
blackened trunks proba-
bly from the eruption of
Cinder Cone in the late
1500's. There are also
Ponderosa and Jeffrey
Pine further away from
the Fantastic Lava Flow
with blackened trunks all
facing the Lava Flow
which indicates that they
were far enough away to
survive.

The trail departs
from the self-guiding na-
ture trail at guide marker
23, and continues in a
westerly direction passing Cinder Cone on its north side. After 1.5 miles from the
trailhead, there is a trail junction with Snag Lake 2.0 miles (3.2 km), and Lower
Twin Lake 3.6 miles (5.8 km) to the left. Badger Flat 5.0 miles (8.0 km), Hat Lake
11.0 miles (17.8 km) straight ahead. Since the trail is via the Nobles Emigrant
Trail, it continues straight ahead. Two tenths of a mile further, there is another
trail junction to Juniper Lake, Warner Valley, Rainbow Lake, and Lower Twin Lake
to the left. However, the trail via Nobles Emigrant Trail continues straight ahead.
Don't be confused by the distances on the wood signs. They are rounded to the
nearest half mile. The metal signs are accurate to .1 of a mile.) As you hike

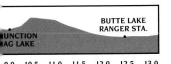

through the Cinder Desert with the wagon wheel
ruts, you expect to see the bones of dead oxen
and perhaps a shallow grave or two.

As the trail continues in a westerly direction, it re-enters a forest of mostly Lodgepole Pine. Ground cover reapppears in the form of Rabbit Brush, Pennyroyal, and Squaw Carpet. Some of the rocks in the wagon ruts have scars probably made by the wagon wheels. The trail enters a dense wet Lodgepole Pine forest with wildflowers. It makes a pleasant contrast with the Cinder Desert that the trail has just crossed. There are many birds, mostly mountain chickadees. A short distance further brings a trail junction with Cinder Cone 3.1 miles (5.0 km) back, Badger Flat 2.6 miles (4.1 km) ahead, Lower Twin Lake 2.8 miles (4.4 km) to the left (south). Immigrant trails, in addition to skirting natural obstacles, had to have periodic places along the way that provided water and pasture for the animals, and obviously, Badger Flat was one of those. Immigrant trails make good trails for horseback riding.

After .5 of a mile, Fairfield Peak is visible to the front. The trail remains level through an open forest of Lodgepole Pine, and as it continues, Red Fir joins along with Western White Pine. Wildflowers include Rabbit Brush, Blue Penstemon, Pennyroyal, Pussy Paws, and Lupine. After 2.4 miles (3.9 km) from the previous trail junction, there is the trail junction with the trail to the right to Feather Lake 1.1 miles (1.8 km), Silver Lake 1.5 miles (2.5 km), Cluster Lake 2.0 miles (3.2 km), Badger Flat 4.6 miles (7.4 km), and back to Soap Lake 3.5 miles (5.7 km). From the junction, the trail continues in a southerly direction through a pretty forest. One tenth of a mile from the junction, there is an old C.C.C. cabin on the left. Another .1 of a mile brings the north edge of Lower Twin Lake. At the time of writing, the trail around the north edge of the lake was not marked. The best swimming is at a small beach at this spot. Half way around the east side of the lake, there is a trail junction back to the north, Cluster Lake 2.6 miles (4.1 km), Badger Flat 5.2 miles (8.3 km), straight ahead Upper Twin Lake .7 of a mile (1.1 km), Horseshoe Lake 3.3 miles (5.4 km), Summit Lake 4.3 miles (6.9 km), Warner Valley 7.3 miles (11.8 km). To the left is Rainbow Lake .5 of a mile (.9 km), Snag Lake 2.7 miles (4.4 km), Cinder Cone 3.9 miles (6.3 km), Butte Lake 5.2 miles (8.4 km).

After an initial ascent of .1 of a mile, the trail levels and proceeds through a pretty, open forest of Red Fir, Lodgepole and Western White Pine with Pennyroyal and Silver Leaf Lupine for ground cover. The trail descends .1 of a mile into Rainbow Lake. The trail follows around its north edge for .3 of a mile to another trail junction. To the right, Snag Lake is 1.9 miles (3.1 km). To the left, Cinder Cone 3.1 miles (5.0 km), Butte Lake 4.4 miles (7.1 km), and back Lower Twin .8 of a mile (1.3 km), Summit Lake 5.1 miles (8.2 km). The trail continues in a northeasterly direction, rising steeply for .1 of a mile, then levels. The forest is mainly open with Red Fir, and the ground goes back to cinders. After .9 of a mile from Rainbow Lake, the trail starts a moderate to steep descent which continues all the way to Cinder Cone. Prospect Peak is visible to the front, and Cinder Cone also comes into view. After 2.1 miles from Rainbow Lake there is a trail junction with Summit Lake back 7.3 miles (11.7 km), to the right Snag Lake 1.5 miles (2.5 km), Horseshoe Lake 5.7 miles (9.1 km), Juniper Lake 6.7 miles (10.7 km). The trail continues to another trail junction with Butte Lake 1.6 miles ahead, then rejoins the Nobles Emigrant Trail, thus completing the loop.

# Butte Lake

*Butte Lake to Widow Lake and Return*

**TRAILHEAD:** Butte Lake parking area .2 of a mile east of the ranger station

**FEATURES:** Forest and lakes

**DISTANCE:** 3.6 miles (5.8 km) one way. Sign at trailhead reads Head of Butte Lake 2.2 miles (3.6 km), Widow Lake 3.6 miles (5.8 km), Snag Lake 5.0 miles (8.0 km), Horseshoe Lake 9.1 miles (14.6 km), Juniper Lake 9.3 miles (15.0 km), Jakey Lake 9.6 miles (15.4 km).

**TIME:** Allow 4½ hours

**WILDLIFE:** Deer, geese, cormorants, ducks, Cooper's hawk, whistling swan

**HISTORY:** The origin of the name Widow Lake is unknown.

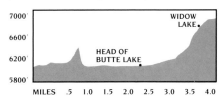

ne tenth of a mile from the start, the trail forks with the main trail going to the
't away from the lake. The trail to the right follows the edge of the lake. The
il along the edge of the lake provides views of Cinder Cone to the west, and
t. Hoffman and Red Cinder Cone to the south. After .7 of a mile along the
wer trail, the path follows a series of steep switchbacks in order to cross above
'ockslide. I would recommend the easier main trail. Either way from the top of
e rockslide, the trail descends steeply on a rocky "watch-your-step" path for
of a mile to lake level of the northeast corner of the lake. It crosses Butte

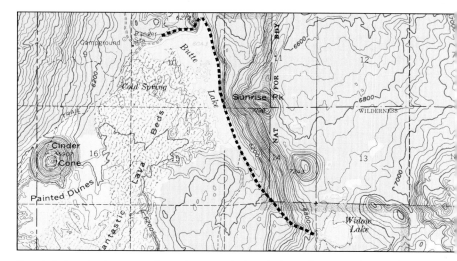

Creek, joins the horse trail, and proceeds level along the east shore. The forest is mainly Ponderosa and Jeffrey Pine with ground cover of Manzanita. The trail surface up to this point is volcanic cinders similar to walking in deep sand, but at this point, the trail becomes firmer which makes walking easier. There are excellent views of Cinder Cone and as the trail continues further south, Lassen comes in view. In the early morning, it's a photographer's bonanza. Yellow wildflowers in bloom consist of Bloomer's Golden Bush.

One tenth of a mile past the lake, there is a trail junction with the trail to the right going to Snag Lake 2.7 miles (4.3 km), Horseshoe Lake 6.9 miles (11.0 km), Juniper Lake 7.1 miles (11.4 km), Jakey Lake 7.3 miles (11.8 km). To the left is Widow Lake 1.4 miles (2.2 km). Jakey Lake is also accessible via Widow Lake and Red Cinder Cone 7.4 miles. For the next .4 of a mile, the trail ascends gradually with a forest of Lodgepole Pine which lacks the beauty of a Ponderosa stand. The forest opens and regains its beauty. At this point, the trail ascends moderately to the left, crossing an intermittent stream bed. There is a footpath to the right, and if you are an experienced hiker, you may want to deviate from the main trail following a level shot to the right front for .3 or .4 of a mile. This is one of the most beautiful sections of forest of magnificent Jeffrey Pine in the Park.

Returning to the main trail, it ascends moderately for .5 of a mile, passing through a fern meadow with wildflowers, and then climbs steeply to Widow Lake adjacent to a talus rock slope on the left for another .5 of a mile. When arriving at the trail marker indicating Widow Lake, one senses disappointment at the small green lakelet, but Widow Lake can be seen behind it, and in a little over .1 of a mile, the lake is before you with its beautiful turquoise color. Its grassy edge makes it easy to walk around. There are campsites all around, and the swimming is excellent, even if it is a little muddy on the bottom. Fishing is questionable, but there are small fish in the lake. Return the same way.

7 # Butte Lake
*Prospect Peak*

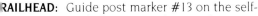

| | | |
|---|---|---|
| **TRAILHEAD:** | Guide post marker #13 on the self-guided nature trail to Cinder Cone | |
| **FEATURES:** | Views, forest, volcanic rock | |
| **DISTANCE:** | 2.8 miles (4.4 km) | |
| **TIME:** | Allow 4 hours | |
| **HISTORY:** | Reputedly named because of extensive prospecting for minerals, which was unsuccessful. Sometimes called East Prospect Peak to | |

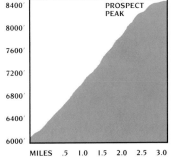

distinguish it from West Prospect Peak, a similar peak adjacent to it on its West side. There were fire lookouts on both Prospect and West Prospect Peaks. It has also been called "Sand Butte" because of the extensive area of black cinders on its south and east slopes. "Black Butte" has also been used as a name.

**AUTHOR'S COMMENTS:** There is no water available. Though the views from the top of East Prospect Peak are enjoyable, they do not, in my opinion, compare to those from Lassen Peak, Brokeoff, Mt. Harkness or Inspiration Point. Because of this and the tiring climb, I would not give this hike a high priority if limited for time.

Initially, the trail climbs gradually for .2 of a mile through an open forest of Ponderosa and Jeffrey Pine in a westerly direction, then it steepens. White Fir joins the forest, which remains open with a peaceful feel to it. The relentless climb and the loose cinders combine to make the climb very tiring, even for conditioned hikers. Ground cover is pine needles over cinders. Approximately .5 of a mile from the start, Red Fir, Green Leaf and Pinemat Manzanita make their appearance. The trail is easily defined. After approximately 1.2 miles, there is a draw to the right, which looks like it has been scooped out by a glacier, and there are piles of lava rocks in it. As the trail gains elevation, Western White Pine combined with a carpet of Pinemat Manzanita add beauty to the forest. The trail becomes very steep and skirts a number of lava flow outcroppings on the right. Prospect Peak is a shield volcano. Near the top, the timber becomes sparse, which provides views of Cinder Cone, Snag and Butte lakes to the southeast. Mountain Hemlock is present as well as White Bark Pine with its twisted gnarled trunks. After reaching the top, the trail continues around to the north side of the Cone. There are the remains of an abandoned lookout, and good views, particularly of Lassen Peak.

# 38 Butte L./Cinder Cone

**TRAILHEAD:** Butte Lake Ranger Station

**FEATURES:** Self-guiding nature trail, volcanic phenomena, scenic views, forest

**DISTANCE:** 1.4 miles (2.2 km) to the base of Cinder Cone, .5 of a mile (.8 km) further to the top.

**TIME:** Allow 2½ hours or 3 hours if you return by loop trail

**WILDLIFE:** Pika

**HISTORY:** Cinder Cone is a very apt name describing a nearly perfect cone mountain of cinders. It is remarkably symmetrical with a triple rim. It is about 700 feet high , and was last active in the late 1600's. At this time it poured a series of basalt lava flows from its base into Butte Lake. Other names given this volcano have been "Cinder Butte," " Black Butte," and merely "Volcano."

**AUTHOR'S COMMENTS:** From the top of Cinder Cone, the trail to Snag Lake looks like a short, easy hike. Don't be misled, because of the deep cinders and the distance, it is not as easy as it looks.

This is another nature trail with leaflets available at the trailhead which describe in detail the 44 points of interest along the trail. This information has been duplicated on page 83 with the exception of the pictures. At the trail marker #3, the trail sign indicates Cinder Cone 1.2 miles (2.0 km), Snag Lake 3.4 miles (5.6 km), Lower Twin Lake 4.9 miles (7.8 km), Horseshoe Lake 7.5 miles (12.2 km), Juniper Lake 8.5 miles (13.8 km), Summit Lake 9.2 miles (14.8 km), Hat Lake 12.3 miles (19 8 km), The trail takes a gradual ascent through a pleasant forest of Ponderosa and Jeffrey Pine. At trail marker #11, there is a footpath leading to Cold Spring. In late fall, the spring may be dry, but cold air can be felt. In the early days before electricity, Park Rangers used the cold air vents for their refrigeration. At marker #13, the trail to Prospect Peak branches to the right 2.8 miles (4.4 km). At marker #25, the trail ascends Cinder Cone. The cinders are loose and it is like walking in sand. The trail climbs a vertical 700 feet, however, by resting when needed, the trail is not difficult. Small children may have a problem. On top of the rim, there are impressive panoramic views in all directions explained in detail by the nature leaflet. The trail proceeds to the right, circles the west rim, and descends into the crater. Climbing out, the trail circles the remaining rim and descends the south side, eventually circling to the west and north, where it joins the trail from Snag Lake to Butte Lake. You can choose to return via this loop, or by the way you came.

Hiking Trails of Lasser

# 39 Butte L./Bathtub Lake

**TRAILHEAD:** Parking and picnic area. Two tenths of a mile east of the Butte Lake Ranger Station

**FEATURES:** Lake, forest, wildflowers

**DISTANCE:** .4 of a mile (.7 km)

**TIME:** Allow 45 minutes to 1 hour

**TOPOGRAPHY:** Rises approximately 80 vertical feet and descends approximately 120 vertical feet

**HISTORY:** *Butte Lake:* Name appears on maps commencing in 1883. It probably stemmed from the early names of Cinder Butte or Black Butte originally given to Cinder Cone. The lake was also named "Lake Bidwell" after General John Bidwell of Chico fame by map maker J. S. Diller.
*Bathtub Lake:* The name was suggested in 1930 by Ranger Harlan Lee because of the small regular shape and smooth cinder bottoms of these lakes. The smaller lake is referred to as "Small Bathtub Lake." At one time, the lakes were called "Twin Lakes."

**AUTHOR'S COMMENTS:** This is a nice hike for children or a pleasant way to walk-off dinner. It's not nearly as strenuous as Cinder Cone or Prospect Peak, and offers an alternative. Because of its waters and smooth bottom, Bathtub Lake is considered one of the best swimming lakes in the Park.

For the first .1 of a mile, the trail ascends a moderately steep cinder path in a forest of Ponderosa and Jeffrey Pine. The trail levels, and after .3 of a mile, there is a small lakelet. The trail forks left and descends steeply .1 of a mile to Bathtub Lake. Both lakes provide warm swimming. It's a short (10 min.) hike around Bathtub Lake and there are interesting rock formations exhibiting glacier polish and striations. White Fir insists upon some space, and there are wildflowers along its shore. There are no fish in either lake, and camping is not allowed. As the trail enters the lake, there is a Ponderosa Pine growing out of a rock. This is not unusual for Juniper, but it's rare for Ponderosa. Return the same way.

# 40 Butte Lake

*Butte Lake Campground to Snag Lake via east shore of Butte Lake and return via the west shore of Snag Lake*

**TRAILHEAD:** Butte Lake parking lot .2 of a mile east of Ranger Station

**FEATURES:** Lakes, forest, wildlife, wildflowers and volcanic phenomena

**DISTANCE:** Snag Lake 5.0 miles (8.0 km), Juniper Lake Trail 6.5 miles (10.5 km) return via Cinder Cone 12.6 miles (20.4 km) total

**TIME:** Allow 7 hours

**WILDLIFE:** Deer (including a buck), geese, swan

**HISTORY:** *Snag Lake:* formed by the basaltic lava flows from Cinder Cone damming Grassy Creek. The resulting lake drowned the forest and left many dead trunks or snags. Eventually, these have fallen so that few are still standing.

Initially, the hike is the same as described on page 65, "Butte Lake to Widow Lake." From the trail junction sign at the head of Butte Lake, Widow Lake is 1.4 miles (2.2 km) to the left, Jakey Lake 7.3 miles (11.8 km), Snag Lake 2.7 miles, Horseshoe Lake 6.9 miles and Juniper Lake 7.1 miles to the right. The mostly level trail proceeds through an uninspiring moderately open forest of Lodgepole Pine. The ground cover is Balsam Root, grass, Bloomer's Yellow Bush, and wildflowers with scattered Manzanita and lots of dead snags. Approximately 1.4 miles past the trail junction, there is an impressive stand of Jeffrey Pine. In another .7 of a mile, the trail starts its gradual descent into Snag Lake. There are some beautiful Jeffrey Pine along here also. In another .4 of a mile, the trail enters a grove of Aspen, and .1 of a mile further, the lake is in view. The trail swings to the left and skirts the east side of Snag Lake. The forest is Aspen and pleasant change. As the trail turns west around the south side of Snag Lake, the Aspen give way to a Lodgepole Pine and Fir forest. The water level in Snag Lake varies from year to year. In dry years, the lake is small compared to its basin. Cinder Cone and Prospect Peak are in view to the north. There is a sandy beach along the south shore, good for swimming. There are a number of nice camp spots, and a series of small springs flow into the lake. There are many wildflowers.

Four and three tenths miles (6.9 km) from Butte Lake there is a trail junc

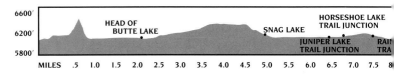

on with Juniper Lake 2.9 miles (4.6 km), Jakey Lake 3.1 miles (5.0 km) to the left, and straight ahead Horseshoe Lake 2.6 miles (4.2 km), Lower Twin Lake 3.7 miles (5.9 km), Cinder Cone 4.7 miles (7.6 km). The trail continues level, crossing additional springs. The forest continues to be mainly Lodgepole Pine. One tenth of a mile past the trail junction to Juniper Lake, a footbridge crosses Grassy Creek. After crossing the footbridge, the forest opens and appears drier and continues to be mainly Lodgepole Pine. The trail forks .3 of a mile further, with the right fork going to Butte Lake Ranger Station via Cinder Cone 5.7 miles (9.2 km), Rainbow Lake 2.5 miles (4.0 km), Lower Twin Lake 3.3 miles (5.3 km). The left-hand fork goes to Horseshoe Lake 2.2 miles (3.6 km), Juniper Lake via Horseshoe Lake .7 miles (5.9 km). The trail is level and proceeds northerly along the west side of Snag Lake. After .6 of a mile, there is a trail junction to the left with Rainbow Lake 1.9 miles (3.1 km), Lower Twin Lake 2.7 miles (4.4 km), Summit Lake 7.0 miles (11.3 km). Straight ahead is Cinder Cone 3.8 miles (6.1 km), Butte Lake 5.1 miles (8.3 km). Back is Horseshoe Lake 2.8 miles (4.5 km), Juniper Lake 3.8 miles (6.1 km). Mt. Hoffman is visible from this point, and you can shake hands with a monster Jeffrey Pine. There are additional campsites along the west shore. The best swimming is more to the north, where the bottom is firmer and the water deeper.

The trail continues northerly along the west edge of the lake. As it leaves the north edge of Snag Lake, it starts ascending moderately and continues to ascend along the western edge of the Fantastic Lava Bed. The trail bottom is volcanic cinders twenty feet deep for the remainder of the hike. It's similar to walking in deep sand, and is tiring. After .3 of a mile, the trail levels, and at this point you can observe Lodgepole Pine growing out of the Lava Beds. The trail has a series of ups and downs, with the ups being quite noticeable in the thick cinders. The trail enters a large desert of volcanic cinders, and swings east to the north of Cinder Cone and the Fantastic Lava Beds. The skeletons of old trees can be seen lying on the cinders. It seems like Death Valley.

Two and nine tenths miles from the last trail junction marker there is another marker with Snag Lake 1.5 miles (2.5 km) back, Horseshoe Lake 5.7 miles (9.1 km) back, Juniper Lake 6.7 miles (10.7 km) back. To the left rear, Rainbow Lake 2.1 miles (3.4 km), Lower Twin Lake 3.0 miles (4.8 km), Summit Lake 7.3 miles (11.7 km). In another .5 of a mile, there is another trail junction to Snag Lake .0 miles and Lower Twin Lake 3.5 miles to the rear. Badger Flat is 4.5 miles, Hat Lake 11.0 miles to the west, and Butte Lake is 2.0 miles straight ahead. In another .4 of a mile, another trail junction sign with Badger Flat 5.0 miles (8.0 km), Hat Lake 11.0 miles (17.8 km), Butte Lake 1.6 miles (2.6 km), Snag Lake .1 miles (3.4 km). The trail continues along the north edge of Cinder Cone through a volcanic bomb field to another trail sign indicating "Top of Cinder Cone and Bypass." The last 1.4 miles is downhill through a pleasant forest of Jeffrey Pine; part of the self-guiding nature trail from the Butte Lake Campground to Cinder Cone. At nature trail post #13, the trail to Prospect Peak branches off to the left. To the right is a trail marked to Cold Spring at the base of the Fantastic Lava Beds. The trail continues along the nature trail to the Ranger Station.

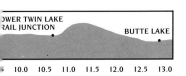

LOWER TWIN LAKE
TRAIL JUNCTION

BUTTE LAKE

10.0  10.5  11.0  11.5  12.0  12.5  13.0

# 41 Pacific Crest Trail
*North to South in Park*

**TRAILHEAD:** North approximately 4.3 miles from sign marker #41 on the Nobles Emigrant Trail; south, Little Willow Lake

**FEATURES:** Famous trail, lakes, hydrothermal activity, wildflowers, and forest.

**DISTANCE:** The Pacific Crest Trail extends from Canada to Mexico approximately 2,600 miles. From its northern entrance into the park to Badger Flat 1.7 miles (2.8 km), Soap Lake 3.2 miles (5.2 km), Emigrant Trail junction to Lower Twin Lake 4.3 miles (7.0 km), Lower Twin Lake 7.1 miles (11.5 km), Corral Meadow 11.7 miles (19.0 km), Warner Valley Campground 14.1 miles (22.8 km), southern boundary 18.4 miles (29.8 km).

**TOPOGRAPHY:** See maps for trails mentioned below

**TIME:** Allow 2 days (1 night overnight)

**WILDLIFE:** Deer (bucks & does), many birds including hawk and eagle, bear, mountain quail, grouse

**AUTHOR'S COMMENTS:** The Pacific Crest Trail is best hiked in segments related to the following hikes:
- Hat Lake to Soap Lake, page 29
- Butte Lake to Lower Twin Lake, return via Cinder Cone and Nobles Emigrant Trail, return via Rainbow Lake, page 62
- Juniper Lake to Lower Twin Lake via Cameron Meadow and Horseshoe Lake, return via Grassy Swale Creek, page 49
- Summit Lake to Lower Twin Lake via Grassy Swale Creek, page
- Drakesbad to Kings Creek via Sifford Lakes, return via Kings Creek Falls and Corral Meadow, page 42
- Kelly Camp to Corral Meadow, return to Warner Valley Campground via Flatiron Ridge, page 41
- Drakesbad to Terminal Geyser Loop via Boiling Springs and Little Willow Lake, page 47

The Pacific Crest Trail crosses the northern boundary of the Park approximately .3 of a mile before it joins the Nobles Emigrant Trail at the junction. At the time of writing, a sign post was all that was left of the sign. There is a Pacific Crest Trail tag nailed to a Jeffrey Pine. After .3 of a mile further, the trail levels, and the forest goes back to a repetitious forest of Lodgepole Pine. Ground cover is predominately Bloomer's Golden Bush. Two tenths of a mile before the trail junction, Badger Flat is visible to the right. At the Badger Flat trail junction, Hat Lake back 6.1 miles (8.7 km), straight ahead Butte Lake 6.6 miles (10.6 km), to the right (south) Cluster Lake 2.0 miles (3.3 km), Big Bear Lake 3.2 miles (5.1 km), Lower Twin Lake 5.0 miles (8.0 km), Summit Lake 6.8 miles (10.9 km). Continuing straight ahead, the trail ascends moderately through the continuing forest of mostly Lodgepole Pine for .2 of a mile, then more or less levels. It continues in an easterly direction for 1.3 miles further to Soap Lake on the right (south).

In another 1.1 miles, there is a trail junction with Lower Twin Lake to the right (south) 2.8 miles (4.4 km). Ahead is Cinder Cone 3.1 miles (5.0 km), and Badger Flat to the rear 2.6 miles (4.1 km). The trail proceeds south on to Lower Twin Lake, and after .5 of a mile, Fairfield Peak is visible to the front. The trail remains level through an open forest of Lodgepole Pine, and as it continues, Red Fir joins along with Western White Pine. Wildflowers include Rabbit Brush, Blue Penstemon, Pennyroyal, Pussy Paws, and Lupine. After 2.4 miles (3.9 km) from the previous trail junction, there is the trail junction with the trail to the right to Feather Lake 1.1 miles (1.8 km), Silver Lake 1.5 miles (2.5 km), Cluster Lake 2.0 miles (3.2 km), Badger Flat 4.6 miles (7.4 km), and back, Soap Lake 3.5 miles (5.7 km).

From the junction, the trail continues in a southerly direction through a pretty forest. One tenth of a mile from the junction, there is an old C.C.C. cabin on the left. Another .1 of a mile brings the north edge of Lower Twin Lake. At the time of writing, the trail around the north edge of the lake is not marked. The best swimming is at a small beach at this spot. Halfway around the east side of the lake, there is a trail junction back to the north, Cluster Lake 2.6 miles (4.1 km), Badger Flat 5.2 miles (8.3 km), straight ahead Upper Twin Lake .7 of a mile (1.1 km), Horseshoe Lake 3.3 miles (5.4 km), Summit Lake 4.3 miles (6.9 km), Warner Valley 7.3 miles (11.8 km). To the left (east) is Rainbow Lake .5 of a mile (.9 km), Snag Lake 2.7 miles (4.4 km), Cinder Cone 3.9 miles (6.3 km), Butte Lake 5.2 miles (8.4 km). The level trail continues around the east side of Lower Twin Lake to the trail junction to Upper Twin Lake .5 of a mile, and Summit Lake 4.1 miles to the right (west), to the left Snag Lake 3.0 miles, Cinder Cone 4.2 miles, Badger Flat 5.4 miles and Butte Lake 5.5 miles. In .6 of a mile, the level trail passes on the west side of Swan Lake. Three tenths of a mile past Swan Lake, the trail forks with the left (east) trail going to Horseshoe Lake 2.2 miles. There is an outstanding stand of Red Fir at this trail junction. The forest changes into Lodgepole Pine and there is a good display of wildflowers that like it dry, including Pussy Paws, Blue Penstemon, Silverleaf Lupine, Sky Rocket Gilia, and Indian Paint Brush. The trail parallels the northwest side of Grassy Swale Creek and after another 1.3 miles from the previous trail junction, there is another junction with Horseshoe Lake 2.0 miles to the left (south) and back Lower Twin Lake 2.0 miles, Cinder Cone 6.4 miles, and Butte Lake 7.7 miles. Ahead is Corral Meadow 2.4 miles. The trail remains level through a peaceful forest and meadow with many birds and deer.

After approximately 1.2 miles from the junction, the trail crosses Grassy Swale Creek and there are many wildflowers that like it wet. The trail parallels Grassy Swale Creek on its southwest side, proceeding through a mountain meadow containing Wild Lilac bushes. The trail descends gradually, and then steepens into the Kings Creek drainage. The trail crosses Kings Creek and after approximately 1.2 miles from crossing Grassy Swale Creek, it arrives at Corral Meadow. There is a junction with Warner Valley 2.4 miles and Kelly Camp 4.0 miles left (south). Back is Horseshoe Lake 4.5 miles, Lower Twin Lake 4.6 miles, Cinder Cone 8.8 miles and Butte Lake 10.1 miles. Proceeding to Warner Valley, the trail is mostly level for .2 of a mile where the trail forks with the left-hand going to Kelly Camp and the right to Warner Valley 2.2 miles. The trail rises moderately to steeply for .8 of a mile, then becomes level, travelling through a dense forest of Red and White Fir. It then descends gradually for .3 of a mile. When it levels, the forest is open and has a peaceful feel to it.

One and five tenths miles from Corral Meadow, there is a trail junction to the right (west) with the trail to Sifford Lakes 2.3 miles, Kings Creek Falls 2.6 miles, and Kings Creek Meadows 3.6 miles. For the last mile, the trail descends into Warner Valley. There are majestic cliffs and a wonderful panorama of Warner Valley. From the Warner Valley Campground, the trail descends to the road to Drakesbad. Follow the road to the right (west) for .2 of a mile to the parking lot. At the trailhead, there are self-guiding nature leaflets available with numbered points of interest. For the first .1 of a mile, the trail is mainly level, paralleling Hot Springs Creek. As it crosses the creek, it starts to ascend gradually. There are wildflowers including Queen Anne's Lace, Monkey Flower, Aster, and Bull Thistle. After .4 of a mile, the trail forks with the right fork going to Devils Kitchen 1.8 miles, and the left going to Boiling Springs Lake, Drake Lake and Terminal Geyser. Fifty feet further, the trail forks again, the trail to the right going to Drake Lake 1.9 miles and the left continuing to Boiling Springs Lake and Terminal Geyser. Ground cover is sparse and the forest consists of Lodgepole Pine, Incense Cedar, White and Red Fir. There is another fork in the trail .7 of a mile from the start at guide marker #16 with the left going to Terminal Geyser (2.0 miles) and the right to the Boiling Springs Lake circuit. The route goes right and will return here after completing the loop. Two tenths of a mile further is Boiling Springs Lake.

The self-guiding nature trail continues around the right side of the lake and the trail again forks at self-guiding marker #33 with Terminal Geyser, 1.5 miles to the right (south). From this junction, the trail to Terminal Geyser climbs steeply and then has a series of moderate rises. The forest has some magnificent Incense Cedar and Jeffrey Pine. Two tenths of a mile before Terminal Geyser, the trail to Little Willow Lake forks to the right 1.1 miles. Little Willow Lake is the southern point of the Pacific Crest Trail in Lassen Park. This junction is also where the loop joins from the trail mentioned .7 of a mile from the start. The trail to Little Willow Lake is marked with gray diagonal markers as well as the Pacific Crest Trail markers, instead of the normal yellow discs. After approximately .2 of a mile, the forest opens and Mt. Harkness is in view to the left (west). The trail has a series of undulations, ascending approximately 240 vertical feet. It then descends steeply approximately .3 of a mile 240 vertical feet. Little Willow Lake is a good example of the transition that all Lassen Park lakes are gradually making from lake to mountain meadow. Presently, it is more like a wet green marsh and it offers no fishing or swimming. There is a Pacific Crest Trail register at the lake. The trail continues around the east side of the lake and then swings southeasterly to the southern boundary of the Park.

# Bumpass Hell

Self-guiding Nature Trail

*The brochure for this trail has been rewritten and can be found at Park Service Headquarters or the trail-head.*

About eleven thousand years ago, Lassen Peak shoved its way through the side of Mt. Tehama. The world's largest plug dome volcano probably rose to its full height in five short years.

2 Glaciers, tremendous bodies of ice hundreds of feet thick, passed this way, gouging, scratching and polishing these solid lavas.

3 Mt. Conard, Brokeoff Mountain, Mt. Diller, Pilot Pinnacle, and the grouund upon which you stand are remains of the once mighty Mt. Tehama, a composite volcano similar to Mt. Shasta.

A million years in the building, Tehama was then largely destroyed, perhaps in a few thousands of years. First volcanic activity weakened the areas on each side of Diamond Peak, then streams and glaciers carved them out to form valleys.

4 You know you are high in the mountains when you see a whitebark pine tree. Only a few specimens live here at 8,200' but whitebark pine is the only tree that can survive the harsh wind and snow conditions that prevail 1,000' higher on Lassen Peak. These high elevation habitats are the result of volcanic mountain building.

5 Recent glacial activity dimpled Lassen's steep slopes and help us date the peak. Older than Lassen, 110-feet-deep Lake Helen was scooped out by the same enormous glaciers that modified Mt. Tehama.

6 The boulder sitting across the canyon just to the left of the parking area demonstrates the power of a glacier. This "glacial erratic" was carried along in the ice flow and left perched on the ridge when the ice melted.

7 Volcanic landscapes contain steep terrain and porous rocks. Water does not stay on the surface because it either drains off or seeps quickly into the ground to reappear elsewhere as a spring. East Sulphur Creek originates at the bottom of the canyon as seepage from Lake Helen and surrounding areas.

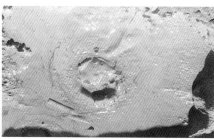

**8** As lava cools and contracts, it forms a system of parallel cracks, known as jointing. Water then seeps into these cracks, freezes, and wedges blocks of rock loose to tumble and form talus slopes. These barren slopes look forbidding to us, but to the pika (or cony) they make an ideal home. Listen for the harsh, high-pitched call of these strange-looking small relatives of the rabbit.

**9** Notice especially on the slopes below you how silverleaf lupine has adjusted to living on high mountain slopes. Silvery hairs on the leaves reflect the intense ultraviolet radiation of this thin atmosphere. They also help maintain stable temperature and moisture conditions around the leaf by trapping a layer of air.

Pikas collect lupines and dry them in "haystacks" before storing them deep in the loose rocks for winter food.

**10** Mountain hemlock is the predominant tree of this area. Short waxy needles and a spreading root system help it to grow on these dry slopes. Notice how the trees tend to grow in clumps in order to survive the struggle against powerful winter winds and deep snow.

**11** As is common among plants that grow in this fierce environment, pinemat manzanita hugs the ground. Its vertical waxy leaves help conserve water. Its berries and seeds provide important food for birds and mammals who live here.

**12** Lightning left a calling card here. Lightning storms are frequent near timberline, but because vegetation is sparse, fires do not normally spread far.

**13** All of the mountains in the Cascade Range, including Lassen Peak and Mt. Tehama, are volcanoes. However, the Sierra Nevada and the Coast Range visible in the distance were formed by different processes. Starting 10 miles south of here, the Sierra Nevada are primarily masses of granite that have been uplifted and tilted. The coastal mountains were largely formed by a squeezing process that folded, buckled, and uplifted them.

**14** Spring comes late and winter early in the high mountains as is evidenced by the very thin growth rings on the trunk of this 400-year-old cut tree.

**15** Bumpass Hell testifies to the existence of a residual mass of cooling lava perhaps 3 miles or so deep in the earth's crust. Bumpass Hell is not one of Mt. Tehama's main vents, but lies on the slope outside the caldera of the former volcano. It just happens that one of the many fissures or faults that riddle the

gion between the Sierra Nevada and the coastal mountains northwest of us
enetrates deep enough here to tap volcanic heat.

5  Three types of lava are visible here. That which forms the rugged wall on the
her side of Bumpass Hell is dacite, the same material that comprises Lassen
eak. Stiff and pasty when molten, it tends to be shoved up as spines rather
an spreading out in a lava flow.

In the distance stands Mt. Harkness, a shield volcano with a small cinder cone
n top. It assumed the shape of a giant Roman shield because its basalt lavas
ere highly fluid when molten.

Mt. Tehama, including Bumpass Hell and the ground upon which you stand,
onsists of andesite which is intermediate between dacite and basalt in
aracteristics. The sequence of flows from magma chambers over vast periods
 time is commonly from basalt to andesite and then dacite.

*  Volcanic rock gives off water when heated. The magma chamber under you is
ving off hot steam and volcanic fumes including hydrogen sulfide which is the
urce of the rotten-egg smell. Surface waters percolate down through cracks in
e earth's crust until they come into contact with the hot steam rising from
e magma chamber or with hot rock above the magma. Then they return to
e surface again as steam. Indeed most of the steam coming from Bumpass
ell originates as surface water. **A short spur trail with numbered sign posts
ads to an interesting boiling spring.**

`  Violent, roaring, hot steam spewing from the "Steam Engine" aptly
emonstrates why Bumpass Hell is called a hydrothermal area (water — heat).
ater boils at 198° F. at this elevation rather than the 212° F. normal at sea level.
owever, this steam can be superheated by several additional degrees because
 was heated under pressure.

)  Although colorful, Bumpass Hell is a barren place. High temperatures
ombine with high concentrations of sulphur compounds and other factors to
eate an environment that is inhospitable to plants and animals. The difference
 the abilities of living forms to tolerate these conditions is clearly illustrated
 bog kalmia, pink heather, and rushes. Notice how bog kalmia and the grass-
e rushes creep down this slope while pink heather is almost entirely restricted
 the bank on the other side of the trail.

)  Andesite lavas decompose readily, but sulfuric acid and hot steam have
eatly speeded up the process to carve out this 16-acre bowl. Surface streams
eding Bumpass Hell influence both the amount of steam produced and the
rength of the acid.

Change is constant in Bumpass Hell and many features now differ from the
ay they were when K. V. Bumpass first viewed them over 100 years ago. Some of
e changes have been sudden while most are the result of slower but persistent
ocesses.

  A vast reservoir of steam, probably several miles in area, feeds these dry
nts or fumaroles and Bumpass Hell's other thermal features. Perhaps
umpass Hell, Boiling Springs Lake, Devil's Kitchen andd Sulphur Works all tap
e same giant reservoir.

  The presence of sufficient water dilutes sulfuric acid and the decomposition
 the lavas is incomplete. Clays such as those percolating in this muddy pool
e then formed.

  The whitish material in this mound is a nonprecious form of opal which results from the complete decomposition of the lava in the absence of plentiful water.

**25** This former pool is an example of the continual changes in an active thermal area. While this pool has dried up, others in Bumpass Hell have enlarged and new ones have formed.

**26** East Pyrite Pool boils violently in spite of the cool stream flowing into it. The black scum and bubbles on the surface contain tiny crystals of iron pyrite or "fools gold," an iron compound which is a product of chemical reactions in thermal waters. When in large pieces fools gold has the gold color and metallic luster from whence it gained its name. Other iron compounds cause the red, yellow and tan colorations in Bumpass Hell.

Lean against the large boulder to the left. The vibrations you feel are probably caused by steam pressure underground.

**27** Mudpots are an intermediate type of thermal feature between hot springs with a plentiful supply of water, and fumaroles which are dry. The force of the steam here is strong enough to splash hot mud and build up a rim creating a "mud volcano."

**28** In 1947 West Pyrite Pool was enlarged by 800 feet when a large portion of the surrounding crust collapsed to create the largest sudden change in topography in Bumpass Hell that has ever been recorded.

**29** Acid, steam, rain and frost will continue to attack these rounded boulders until they too are reduced to a powder or clay.

**30** Yellow sulphur crystals often form on surfaces covered by thin sheets of thermal waters or where hydrogen sulfide hisses from holes in the ground.

**31** Tremendous amounts of energy are released in dramatic form by the "Big Boiler." The flow of energy in nature is continuous, and everything in nature, living or not, is tied to it. As you retrace your steps, reconsider the dramas portrayed along the train in terms of energy flow.

# Boiling Springs Lake

Self-guiding Nature Trail

The brochure for this trail is being rewritten and will be found at Park Service Headquarters or the trailhead.

Most of the trees in this picnic area are lodgepole pine (*Pinus contorta*). Its bark is thin and scaly. The needles occur in bundles of two and are twisted, thus the scientific name "contorta." The cones may remain on the branches for several years.

At the base of this dead tree are the remains of a colony of large red ants. The collection of twigs and pine needles represent a shelter building project of a well developed social system.

Hot Springs Creek is fed partly by natural thermal water from Boiling Springs Lake, Devil's Kitchen and a few hot springs along the trail. However, most of the water comes from a stream above Devil's Kitchen and from cold water springs along the sides of Warner Valley. Further down the valley this stream joins with Kings Creek to form Warner Creek. Watch for the dipper, a small gray bird that feeds in the fast flowing water.

Beavers (*Castor canadensis*) have been active in Warner Valley as can be seen by gnawed trees along stream banks. Look for evidence along the trail. Their home is usually a pile of sticks and mud in a pool behind a dam which they build across a stream. Sometimes they tunnel into a stream bank from an underwater entrance.

White fir (*Abies concolor*) is one of the most common trees to be seen along the trail. Needles grow singly rather than in groups like the pines. The large white fir behind these two young ones is 14.3 feet in circumference, one of the largest you will see in Warner Valley. True fir cones grow straight up like candles and fall apart at maturity while still attached to the branchlets. Thus, you seldom see whole fir cones on the ground.

This exposed slope may look dry and barren in late summer but it is rich with flowers during the early summer. The grayish bare exposure facing you on the opposite slope is composed of mineral deposits from hot springs, some of which are still active. You will see a small hot spring at stake number 8.

Warner Valley was originally formed when stresses within the earth caused a huge block of the crust to sink, creating a steep trough known as a graben. During the Ice Age glaciers moving slowly down from the mountains widened and gouged the trough to form a broad U-shaped valley. You are standing on a rock and gravel slope that was probably deposited by a glacier as a lateral or side moraine. Flatiron Ridge on the other side of the valley is composed of old lava flows, known as flatiron andesite, that were exposed by the glaciers. Stream erosion has played an important part in shaping Warner Valley since the glaciers' retreat.

Several natural hot springs feed this little stream to supply water for the thermal pool at Drakesbad Guest Ranch. The pool is for guests only. The water is heated through contact with hot rocks deep underground. In the 1860's a settler named Edward R. Drake promoted the thermal waters for a health spa or "bad." It remained a private resort until 1958, when the property was purchased by the government and added to the Park. Drakesbad is now operated by the Lassen National Park Company, which also operates Manzanita Lake Lodge, under

National Park Service regulations.

**9** This large incense cedar (*Libocedrus decurrens*) is 22.5 feet in circumference. The reddish bark looks somewhat like that of the giant sequoia, but none of the latter are found in this area. Large sections of the bark were used by Indians to form conical shelters. The wood has an incense-like fragrance.

The trail to the right leads to Drakesbad and Devil's Kitchen. The latter is a fascinating area of violently steaming fumaroles, hot springs and boiling mudpots at the head of Warner Valley.

**10** The broad-leaf shrub here is a Scouler willow (*Salix scouleriana*). Most species of willows grow best in wet meadows or along streams and lakeshores. This one, however, prefers dry places along meadow edges or in open woods. The leaves are wider and rounded on the ends; other species of willows have narrow pointed leaves.

**11** The stream next to the trail is overflow from Boiling Springs Lake and may become dry in midsummer. Notice the whitish mineral deposits from the thermal water on the rocks in the streambed.

**12** Young red fir (*Abies magnifica*) needles are blue-green in color as compared to the yellow-green needles of white fir. This blue-green color suggests the name "silvertip," a name heard at Christmas time. However, trees are never taken from the National Parks for this purpose. Notice the lacy appearance of the branchlets on the taller red fir trees.

**13** Evidences of old fires may be seen in many places in the forest. Long periods without rain cause the forest litter to become extremely flammable. An observer is employed during the summer at a fire lookout station on top of Mt. Harkness, which overlooks Warner Valley and much of the rest of the Park. Fires started by lightning or by careless hikers and campers are reported and extinguished as soon as possible by firefighting crews.

**14** The large Jeffrey pine (*Pinus jeffreyi*) overhead has probably withstood several forest fires in its lifetime. Its thick bark is fairly resistant to light ground fires. When the trunk of the tree is warmed by the sun, you can detect a fragrant vanilla or pineapple odor in the crevices of the bark. The cones are 5 to 10 inches long, usually much larger than those of ponderosa pine.

**15** The yellowish-green growth on the tree trunks is staghorn lichen (*Letharia vulpina*). Actually a specialized combination of species of fungus and alga living together, it does no harm to the trees and grows on dead snags just as well. The green alga utilizes sunlight and moisture to provide food for the plant while the fungus provides support and holds the mass together.

**16** Bears are not common in the Park but have been seen in this vicinity and near Summit and Juniper Lakes. Their tracks are seen occasionally along the trails. Clawed or chewed wooden trail signs also denote their presence.

**17** Fallen and dead standing trees are usually left in place in the National Parks. They provide home sites, food, and shelter for small mammals, insects, and birds. Notice the bark beetle "engravings" on some of the fallen tree trunks. The adult beetles lay their eggs in galleries carved for this purpose. When the larvae develop they carve extensive tunnels in their search for food.

**18** In this dense stand of young white fir (*Abies concolor*), only the most vigorous trees will survive. The weaker ones will eventually be crowded out in their struggle to obtain enough sunlight to survive. Some will die as they become shaded by the faster growing ones.

When a tree such as this white fir is bent over by winter snow, some of the
le branches will replace the dead top. When a top is completely broken off or
ed, one and sometimes two side branches will turn upward, as on the small
e on the other side of the trail.

Look closely at the cross section of this fallen Jeffrey pine trunk. The
ncentric growth rings tell the age of the tree. The fastest and softest growth is
the spring and summer. The slowest and hardest growth is in the autumn and
nter. The harder wood stays in tiny ridges while the softer portion wears away.
e living and growing part of the tree is a thin layer just under the bark. The
ide of a living tree as well as the outer layers of bark are dead. As the tree
pands through growth, the bark splits and cracks, forming patterns typical of
ch kind of tree.

The low shrubs here are pinemat manzanita (*Arctostaphylos nevadensis*). They
dom grow over 10 inches tall. White urn-shaped blossoms appear in
dsummer. Late in the summer the red bark peels off in tiny papery curls, due to
owth and expansion. The berries of manzanita (Spanish for "little apple") are
important food item for wildlife.

You are walking up the slope of Red Mountain. The rock outcrop along the
il is Red Mountain basaltic lava, very poor in silica and relatively rich in iron,
agnesium and other minerals. In contrast, the pink dacite lava of Lassen Peak
d Chaos Crags is rich in silica and poor in the other minerals.

You are about to enter the thermal area of Boiling Springs Lake. The rotten
g odor is hydrogen sulfide from the steam vents. Listen for the thumping of
e bubbling mudpots. The stream
st ahead, dry in midsummer, is
e outlet of the lake. The trail
ntinues across the creek, around
e lake and back to this junction.

The pits you see here are dried-
mudpots that have ceased much
their activity, although some
eam may still be visible.
nderground "plumbing" may have
en partly sealed off by slumping
clay and rock material. As
essures continued to build up,
w channels were opened and the
eam escaped from other vents.

Boiling Springs Lake is
nstantly heated to about 125
grees F. by steam rising through
derground vents and fissures. On
ol days, water vapor may be seen
ing from the lake. During the
mmer, the lake level drops more
an a foot. The exposed mud
ound the edge of the lake then
es and cracks. The shoreline

perimeter is about 2,000 feet. The diameter is about 630 feet.

**26** The yellowish-tan color, normal to the lake, is due to clay, opal and iron oxide particles suspended in the water. The green color seen in the shallow water and wet mud are algae, tiny plants which have adapted to the hot water environment.

**27** White, crusty salts, sometimes seen on the surface, are related to alum and have an astringent sweet-sour taste.

**28** This is one of the few places in the Park where you can see the huckleberry oak (*Quercus vaccinifolia*). It grows as a shrub and has huckleberry-like leaves but bears acorns. It retains green leaves all winter. The acorns are eaten by wildlife.

**29** The noisy steaming fumarole across the lake is the most consistently active thermal area in the vicinity. You may see sizzling "frying pan" activity in the stream delta just this side of the fumarole. Steam escaping from small vents in shallow pools sounds like eggs frying.

**30** The large oblong holes in the dead snag, 20 feet off the trail, were made by pileated woodpeckers (*Dryocopus pileatus*). These crow-sized birds are rarely seen in the Park. They make the holes while searching for the larvae of wood-boring beetles. Their nests are usually built high above the ground in the hollows of trees.

**31** The gully at this end of the lake was formed by storm drainage and melting snow. It is the only inlet stream to the lake and dries up in midsummer. Do not attempt to cross the gully here, the trail crosses safely further upstream.

**32** The swollen appearance of the branchlets of these young red fir trees was caused by  dwarfmistletoe (*Arceuthobium campylopodum*). The small golden-colored growth does not have broad leaves like the common mistletoe used at Christmas time. Seeds left on branches by birds sprout, grow into the tree and live as parasites. This growth prevents the flow of nutrients, causing the swelling and weakening of the branch and will, in time, affect the vitality of the tree.

**33** The trail to the right goes to Terminal Geyser, a small thermal area with a violently steaming fumarole. Little Willow Lake, on the same trail near the Park boundary, nearly dries up in late summer and becomes a wet meadow.

**34** Here is a fine view of Lassen Peak. With binoculars you may be able to spot the trail zig-zagging up the left side of the 10,457-foot mountain. It is a plug dome volcano formed when thick, pasty lava was squeezed up through a vent, like toothpaste from a tube. Reading Peak, just to the right of Lassen Peak, is another plug dome volcano. Bumpass Mountain is the knob just visible on the skyline to the left.

**35** The attractive, tall incense cedar to the right is 18.3 feet in circumference. Shrubs near the trail and around the base of the tree are mountain whitethorn ceanothus (*Ceanothus cordulatus*). Deer browse the leaves in spite of the sharp thorns.

**36** *Turn left here to visit the boiling mudpots. BE EXTREMELY CAREFUL! Do not step too close to the slippery or crumbly edges!* Please help to preserve the mudpots. Anything thrown into them will destroy the natural attraction for other visitors.

**37** A mudpot is a type of hot spring consisting of a shallow pit or cavity filled with hot, generally boiling mud with very little water. The mud may have any degree of consistency up to a thick mush or mortar. Steam and gases from underground fissures come up in large bubbles through the thick mud. As the bubbles break, mud is splattered in all directions to form a rim around the vent.

**38** The mud consists mostly of clay and opal colored by iron oxides and sulphur.

Follow the trail to the left back to stake number 23.

# ¦inder Cone
¦-guiding Nature Trail

*The brochure for this trail may be rewritten and would be found at Park Service Headquarters or the trail-head.*

*…s self-guiding trail leads you through a devastated landscape of recent volcanic activity.*
*…tory and dramatic geologic events are combined as you follow the route of early pioneers as*
*…y worked their way west to the Sacramento Valley. Along the way you pass through a pine*
*…st to the edge of a massive lava flow and then up the slope of Cinder Cone to the rim for a*
*…oramic view of lakes, forests, and mountains. Below you unfold the Fantastic Lava Beds,*
*…nted Dunes, Snag and Butte Lakes, and in the distance Lassen Peak dominates the horizon.*
*…he complete 5-mile round trip takes about 3 hours. It is 1½ miles to the base of Cinder*
*…ne and another 1/2 mile to the top. If you don't want to take the entire trip, we suggest that*
*…¦ walk a little over a mile for a view of the Cinder Cone and then return, making an easy*
*…nd trip of just over 2 miles. We suggest that you carry drinking water.*

¦You have probably already noticed that the ground in the campground and
¦nic area is covered with coarse black cinders. This part of the Park is largely
¦vered by cinders erupted from Cinder Cone, Prospect Peak, Fairfield Peak,
¦d Cinder Cone, and other nearby volcanoes.
¦From this point you can see Butte Lake and part of the Fantastic Lava Beds.
¦u will get closer to and learn more about this lava flow farther along the trail.
¦other trail leads clockwise around the lake and on to Snag Lake.
¦From here to the base of Cinder Cone you will be following part of the Old
¦nigrant Trail which was used during the 1850's as one of the routes to the
¦cramento Valley from the east. William H. Nobles established the trail in 1852
¦ a shorter route than Peter Lassen's trail, which went east and south of the
¦esent Park boundary.
¦Beyond this chain the old trail is used only by hikers as far as Badger Flat. You
¦¦y drive in to Badger Flat on a section of the trail starting near Hat Lake from
¦ Lassen Park Road. Parts of the old trail are still clearly visible between here
¦d the Park entrance at Manzanita Lake.

**5** One of the common trees around Butte Lake is the *lodgepole pine*. Needles are short and grow in groups of 2. The cones may remain on the branches for several years. The bark is thin and scaly. Because the trunks grow tall and straight, they make good poles and cabin logs, hence the name lodgepole.

**6** Needles of this *Jeffrey pine* are much longer than those of the lodgepole and grow in groups of 3. The cones take 2 years to develop and are 5 to 10 inches long when mature. Chickarees, or Douglas squirrels, chew many of the cones apart to get the seeds. Piles of chewed cone scales may be seen at the bases of trees or on a favorite log.

**7** Despite injuries caused by lightning, insects, disease, wind and snow, trees are often able to recover and continue growing. When a tree is bent over by snow or some other factor, chemicals in the tree called *auxins* stimulate the growth on the underside of the trunk. This causes the underside to grow faster than the upper side and the tree will tend to right itself.

**8** The Fantastic Lava Beds consist of blocky lava known as basalt (pronounced 'baa-salt'). It was a thick, pasty, slow-flowing mass, red hot inside. As the flow slowly advanced, the crust, cooling and hardening all the while, was twisted and broken into the blocky mass you see here.

**9** Look at the lava closely; you may see white, glassy bits of quartz. The grayish-green scaly material on the surface of some of the rocks is a plant growth called lichen (like-en). Organic acids secreted by these plants help decompose the rocks and slowly add to the formation of soil.

**10** Lightning or heat from the lava flow may have started fires that scorched these trees. If a tree is not killed by the fire, the growing part just under the bark starts to cover the wound. Small scars are sometimes completely covered. Large wounds are left open to attack by insects and fungi. Notice holes drilled by wood boring beetles.

**11** A short spur trail to the left leads to a pocket of cold water at the edge of the lava flow.

**12** The surface of this pool marks the ground-water level. As the water table lowers in late summer, the pool may become dry. Look and listen for the *pika*. These small, dark brown members of the rabbit family live in this rocky habitat. They gather grasses for winter food.

**13** An old trail to Prospect Peak leads off to the right. It climbs about 2200 feet in 2½ miles.

**14** Trees felled by wind, lightning or other causes slowly decay and return to the soil. Carpenter ants, termites, beetles and fungi all do their part. The insects chew the wood into tiny particles while building their tunnels. Fungi live in the dead wood and slowly decompose the tree.

**15** E*ngraver beetles* chew their tunnels just under the bark of weak or freshly killed trees and leave intricate patterns in the wood. In contrast, the boring beetles make their tunnels deep within the trunk of the tree. Woodpeckers drill holes in search of the insects for food.

**16** The whitish soil at the edge of the lava flow is composed of the remains of countless numbers of tiny microscopic plants called diatoms. They grow in oceans, lakes, and even wet soil. The limey skeletons of the plants accumulate on the floor of a body of water to form diatomaceous earth.

**17** Fantastic Lava Beds are composed of lavas from several eruptions. The most recent flow of 1851 does not appear along this edge but courses down

ιe middle, as you will see when you reach the top of Cinder Cone. Some trees ɾowing in this area at the time of the flows were probably killed by the heat of ιe lava. Dead snags along the edge may be remnants of these trees. They have ϵcome "sand-blasted" through the years by windblown cinders.

**8** Notice that there are great quantities of pine cones under the trees but very ϵw seedlings. The porous cinders and dry summer conditions make it difficult ɔr young trees to get started.

**9** The beautifully symmetrical Cinder Cone, straight ahead, rises 700 feet above s base. It was formed by explosive eruptions which threw volcanic ash and ϲinder from a central vent. Much of the material fell around the vent, building ιe cone. Its shape is relatively undisturbed by water erosion because the ϲorous cinders absorb even the heaviest rainfall.

**0** Small fragments of lava shattered by the explosive force of steam and other ϲases escaping from the vent are called "ash" and "cinder." Even though the ινa may be red hot during eruptions it is not burning as is sometimes thought.

**I** The exposed tree root crossing the trail here is protected by layers of bark ΙΙst as on the trunk. While roots are growing underground they do not normally ϵvelop such thick bark layers. Why are these roots exposed?

**2** A severe storm in October, 1962 blew down a number of trees in this area. Ιotice the shallow root system on this fallen Jeffrey pine. During the storm rain ϿΟsened the soil and cinders, causing the tree to topple. The depression left ʰhere the tree was standing may last for several years before being filled in ϵain.

**3** Even though the shape of Cinder Cone is relatively undisturbed by heavy ΞΙnfall, footprints will remain in the cinders indefinitely.

**4** Tiny particles of white pumice found here were blown by the wind from ΞSsen Peak during the 1914-1921 eruptions. Some blew as far as Reno, Nevada, ΙO miles from the Peak. Pumice is light, frothy lava that was filled with gas Ιbbles before it cooled. The dark brown pumice here blew out of Cinder Cone.

**25**  The slope of Cinder Cone is about 35 degrees, the so-called "angle of repose." Loose cinders cannot stay in place on slopes steeper than this. The climb is relatively easy if you take your time. Rest briefly but often.

**26**  Large rounded boulders at the base of the cone are called volcanic bombs. They were blown out of the vent on top of the cone and rolled down the slope while still hot but already hardened. They are composed of glassy basalt which cooled rapidly.

**27**  Lassen Peak is visible in the distance over the shoulder of Cinder Cone. You are looking at the northeast slope of the Peak that was devastated by a huge mud flow and a "Great Hot Blast" during eruptions in May, 1915. Patches of snow remain on the upper slopes of the Peak all summer.

**28**  Prospect Peak is the rounded shield or Hawaiian-type volcano directly to th right, or northwest. It was built, layer upon layer, by lava flows from relatively mild eruptions like those of many of the Hawaiian volcanoes. The term "shield" comes from its resemblance to a Roman shield. A cinder cone tops Prospect Peak, indicating that its final activity was more explosive. The dense growth of trees on its slopes shows that there has been no activity there in recent years. *The trail leads along the rim to the right.*

**29**  The elevation here is about 6900 feet. You are standing on 1 of 3 crater rims each representing a different eruption. Trees growing just inside the crater are *Scouler willow, western white pine,* and *lodgepole pine.*

**30**  Features in this fine panoramic view are identified in the drawing at the bottom of the leaflet.

**31**  Looking directly down the outside slope of Cinder Cone, you can see the source of the rough black lava flow of 1851. You can trace its path toward Snag Lake, then off to the left, toward Butte Lake. An earlier flow dammed the creek flowing into Butte Lake, forming Snag Lake. Lakes formed in this manner are known as coulee lakes. *From here, take the trail behind you to the center rim and look int the main crater.*

**32**  The vent, or vents, from which all these cinders were blown have been covered with cinders and other material falling and sliding back into the central crater. Future eruptions are not likely from this crater; however, they could brea out from other spots nearby. *Continue along this inner rim and then go back to the outer rim on the first trail to the right.*

**33**  Here is a fine view of most of the Fantastic Lava Beds and Butte Lake to the left. *The trail continues down this side of the cone and around the base to the right. If you prefer, you may return to #29 on the opposite side of the crater and go back down the way yo came up.*

**34**  You are looking over the main part of the Painted Dunes. They were formed during explosive eruptions as cinders fell on top of hot lava flows. Heat and steam rising from the hot rocks oxidized the iron in the cinders, producing the various colors you see here.

**35**  Few plants can grow under the hot, dry conditions of this exposed southern slope. In early summer bright yellow *sulphur flowers* and *blue penstemons* add a bit c color to the otherwise drab cinders.

**36**  Take your time going down this steep slope. It is easy to turn an ankle on th larger rocks. The lava is sharp and rough.

**37**  Trees are slowly invading the cinder-covered Painted Dunes, but very few ca e seen growing in the rough, blocky lava flows.

**8** Just below is the source of the 1851 lava flow. Proceed very carefully over the rough lava to the next stake at the edge of the vent.

**9** Reaching back in the "cave," you can feel cold air. You may even see ice in early summer. Such ice caves are common in lava flows where protected pockets stay cold because there is no air circulation.

**0** You are now at the edge of the Painted Dunes.

**1** Note the abundance of volcanic bombs at the base of the cone. Most of them are gradually falling apart as a result of normal weathering, unequal expansion and contraction caused by freezing and thawing of water that accumulates in cracks, and unequal heating by the sun.

**2** The trail to the left goes around the west side of Fantastic Lava Beds to Snag Lake. *The trail continues to the right.*

**3** These are called breadcrust bombs because of their characteristic surface patterns. Homemade bread that has been lightly cut before baking to allow steam to escape will come out of the oven with a similar appearance, except that the bread should not be black.

**4** You are back on the Old Emigrant Trail. Can you imagine the difficulties the wagon trains had in crossing these fields of loose cinders? Along even rougher parts of the trail, broken wagon parts and discarded utensils have been found.

*Sulphur Flowers*

*These trail guides are reprinted from the guides published by Loomis Museum Association, the cooperating association of Lassen Volcanic National Park.*

## LASSEN PARK

*We don't have Yosemite's Bridal Veil Falls,*
*And Cathedral Rock with sheer granite walls,*
*We don't have Half Dome and El Capitan*
*And we're made to feel like an also-ran.*
*We didn't have Ansel Adams and the Range of Light,*
*Or John Preston with all his foresight.*
*But we have Volcanos, Incense Cedar and Jeffrey Pine,*
*Red and White Fir and Mountain Hemock sublime —*
*But the ironic thing that makes us equal*
*Is what we haven't got, all your damned people!*

*There once was a ranger named Bodine*
*Whose career was at Lassen all the time*
*Each transfer he would refuse*
*All with a different ruse*
*He matured in his job just fine*
*Like a cask of old vintage wine.*
*For Les Bodine — Chief Ranger Lassen Volcanic National Park, Retired*

## WILDFLOWERS

*Some like it wet*
*Some like it dry*
*Some like it low*
*Some like it high*
*Some bloom from spring to late fall*
*Some bloom for days —*
*Or hardly at all*

## COWBOY COFFEE

*Hot cowboy coffee is all I got*
*Handful of grounds in a boiling pot*
*A splash of cold water to settle it out*
*And pour the hot brew from the spout*
*And that's what camping's all about*

## GEORGE

*A hiker named George went swimming bare*
*In a lake he thought was Little Bear.*
*He discovered his mistake*
*At the next lake.*
*Much to his chagrin*
*It was Little Bear he was now in.*
*He said it was plain to see*
*I'll name the first lake after me.*
*Unnamed lakes are getting fewer*
*And the other Lake George is a sewer.*

Hiking Trails of Lass

## HIKING TOGETHER

We were hiking together
Talking and laughing as lovers do
Hiking up a ridge towards a knoll
Through wildflowers, massive rocks
And gnarled juniper trees too
Then before us was a scene
Of beauty infinitely sublime
About the beauty with words
We both could extol
Our eyes met for a miniscule of time
And in that instant of silence
We touched each others soul.


## LIFE'S TRAILS

I was on my way to Heaven, just passed away,
When another old man came by, goin' the same way.
I asked him to rest beside me and enjoy the scene
And have a drink of cold water from my canteen
He thanked me, and I said "Why the look of concern?"
He said "I've had a full life but of Heaven I never did learn,
And I'm worried, do you know what it's like?"
"Dont be afraid old man 'cause you see I hike
I've hiked the trails of Lassen
Hiked them everywhere
And I know what Heaven's like
'Cause I've already been there."

# Index of Hike Destinations

*Deer feeding in Butte Lake*

| | | |
|---|---|---|
| Devil's Kitchen | Drakesbad to Devil's Kitchen via Drake Lake, Return to Warner Valley Campground | Hike |
| Drake Lake | Drakesbad to Devil's Kitchen via Drake Lake | Hike |
| Drakesbad | Drakesbad to Kings Creek via Sifford Lakes, Return via Kings Creek Falls and Corral Meadow | Hike |
| | Drakesbad to Dream Lake | Hike |
| | Drakesbad to Devil's Kitchen via Drake Lake | Hike |
| | Drakesbad to Terminal Geyser via Boiling Springs and Little Willow Lake | Hike |
| Dream Lake | Drakesbad to Dream Lake | Hike |
| Echo Lakes | Summit Lake to Cluster Lakes, Return via Upper Twin and Echo Lakes — Detour to Badger Flat | Hike |
| | Summit Lake to Lower and Upper Twin Lake via Corral Meadow and Grassy Swale, Return via Echo Lake | Hike |
| Emigrant Trail | Butte Lake to Lower Twin Lake via Cinder Cone and Emigrant Trail, Return via Rainbow Lake | Hike |
| Flatiron Ridge | Kelly Camp to Corral Meadow to Warner Valley Campground via Flatiron Ridge | Hike |
| Grassy Swale | Summit Lake to Lower and Upper Twin Lake via Corral Meadow and Grassy Swale, Return via Echo Lake | Hike |
| | Juniper Lake Ranger Station to Lower Twin Lake via Cameron Meadow and Horseshoe Lake Return via Grassy Swale | Hike |
| Hat Lake | Hat Lake to Paradise Meadow | Hike |
| | Hat Lake to Soap Lake | Hike |
| Horseshoe Lake | Juniper Lake Ranger Station to Snag Lake, Return via Horseshoe Lake | Hike |
| | Juniper Lake Ranger Station to Lower Twin Lake via Cameron Meadow and Horseshoe Lake, Return via Grassy Swale | Hike |
| | Juniper Lake Ranger Station to Warner Valley Road via Horseshoe and Indian Lakes | Hike |

*orm clearing over Lassen Peak. Hat Lake to Paradise Meadow*

*Lassen Peak from Reflection Lake*

| | | |
|---|---|---|
| Rainbow Lake | Butte Lake to Lower Twin Lake via Cinder Cone and Emigrant Trail, Return via Rainbow Lake | Hike 3 |
| Red Cinder Cone | Juniper Lake Ranger Station to Butte Lake via Jakey Lake, Red Cinder Cone and Widow Lake | Hike 3 |
| Reflection Lk. | Reflection Lake | Hike 1 |
| Ridge Lakes | Ridge Lakes | Hike 2 |
| Shadow Lake | Terrace, Shadow, and Cliff Lakes to Summit Lake | Hike 7 |
| Sifford Lakes | Sifford Lakes, Return via Bench Lake and Kings Creek Falls | Hike 1 |
| | Drakesbad to Kings Creek via Sifford Lakes, Return via Kings Creek Falls and Corral Meadow | Hike 2 |
| Snag Lake | Juniper Lake Ranger Station to Snag Lake, Return via Horseshoe Lake | Hike 3( |
| | Butte Lake to Snag Lake via the East Shore of Butte Lake, Return via the West Shore of Snag Lake | Hike 4( |
| Soap Lake | Hat Lake to Soap Lake | Hike 1 |
| Soda Lake | Soda Lake | Hike 8 |

# About the Author

George Perkins was born in Chicago, Illinois and graduated from New Trier High School in Winnetka, Illinois. He also graduated from the University of Colorado with a degree in business administration. He enlisted in the Korean War and served with Hawaii's famous 5th regimental combat team. He attended officer candidate school at Fort Riley, Kansas and was commissioned a 2nd Lieutenant in 1952. He along with his family operated the Mineral Lodge and the Lassen Park Ski Area during the fifties and sixties. He has three daughters, Heidi, Lynn and Jody, and four step-daughters, Deidra, Darcee, Jill and Jodie. He and his wife Gail, own and operate The Ski Renter, a chain of ski rental shops in California and Nevada. They summer in Mineral. For comments or information, write Box 129, Mineral, CA 96063

# Bibliography

**king, Touring and History**

esbury, Robert. 1967. *Nobles' Emigrant Trail*. Self published: Sold through Loomis Museum Association (Mineral). 37 p.

enhoff, Elizabeth L. 1970. "Lassen — a page from history." California Division of Mines and Geology, *Mineral Information Service*, v. 23, p. 225-227.

tteson, Stephen H. 1963. *Lassen Trails*. Mineral: Loomis Museum Association. 56p.

hulz, Paul E. 1954. *Indians of Lassen Volcanic National Park and Vicinity*. Mineral: Loomis Museum Association. 176 p.

hulz, Paul E. 1979. *Road Guide to Lassen Volcanic National Park*. Mineral: Loomis Museum Association. 40 p.

ong, Douglas H. 1973. *"These Happy Grounds;" a History of the Lassen Region*. Mineral: Loomis Museum Association. 101 p.

haffer, Jeffrey P. 1981. *Lassen Volcanic National Park and Vicinity*. Wilderness Press. 216 p.

artzlow, Ruby J. 1964. *Lassen, His Life and Legacy*. Mineral: Loomis Museum Association. 90 p.

**ology**

andell, Dwight R., and Donal R. Mullineaux. 1970. *Potential geologic hazards in Lassen Volcanic National Park, California*. Washington: U.S. Geological Survey (unpublished administrative report for National Park Service). 54 p.

andell, Dwight R., and others. 1974. "Chaos Crags eruptions and rockfall-avalanches, Lassen Volcanic National Park, California." U.S. Geological Survey, *Journal of Research*, p. 49-59.

ch, R. H. 1937. "A tree ring calendar for dating volcanic events at Cinder Cone, Lassen National Park, California." *American Journal of Science*, v. 33, no. 194, p. 140-146.

ikeh, Grant, and John C. Eichelberger. 1980. "Eruptions at Chaos Crags, Lassen Volcanic National Park, California." *Journal of Volcanology and Geothermal Research*, v. 7, p. 443-481.

ne, Phillip S. 1975. *The Glacial Geomorphology of the Lassen Volcanic National Park Area*. Berkeley: University of California, Geography Department, Ph.D. Thesis. 224 p.

omis, Benjamin F. 1926. (1971). *Pictorial History of the Lassen Volcano (Eruptions of Lassen Peak)*. Mineral: Loomis Museum Association 96 p.

lliams, Howel. 1932. *Geology of the Lassen Volcanic National Park, California*. Berkeley: University of California, Department of Geological Sciences Bulletin, v. 21, p. 195-385.

**ology**

lne, Robert C. 1966. *Birds of Lassen Volcanic National Park*. Mineral: Loomis Museum Association. 48 p.

lson, Raymond L. 1962. *Trees and Shrubs of Lassen Volcanic National Park*. Mineral: Loomis Museum Association. 1971. 35 p.

owers, MaryAnn and David. *A Field Guide to the Flowers of Lassen Volcanic National Park*.

# Glossary

**Abrasion:** removal by erosion of rock due to friction with other rock fragments that are being moved by running water, glaciers, gravity, coastal waves, or wind.

**Andesite:** an extrusive igneous rock composed mostly of plagioclase feldspar and 25-40 percent ferromagnesians.

**Basalt:** A dark, extrusive igneous rock composed of at least 50 percent plagioclase feldspar, as well as pyroxene and perhaps olivine.

**Bombs** (volcanic): large chunks of lava (larger than 2½ inches (64 mm) ejected from a volcanic vent in a molten (plastic) condition; accumulations of bombs may form agglomerate.

**Caldera:** a large more or less circular depression or basin occupying what was once the summit area of a volcano; it results from the subsidence or collapse of the upper part of a volcano into its own magma chamber.

**Cirque:** an amphitheater-shaped depression at the head of a glacial valley; excavated mainly by glacier plucking and hydrofracturing.

**Composite Volcano:** a large volcanic cone composed of alternating layers of both tephra and lava; usually constructed from andesitic magma (see andesite).

**Crater (volcanic):** the funnel-shaped hollow, usually at the top of a volcano, through which tephra and lava are erupted (cf. caldera).

**Dacite:** an extrusive igneous rock composed mostly of feldspar, plus quartz, minor ferromagnesian minerals, and often a high percentage of glass.

**Dome (volcanic):** a small volcano characterized as a mound of felsic rock which, when erupted, was too viscous to flow and instead piled up around its vent; if the vent is actually sealed by the extrusion, it is called a plug-dome.

**Fault:** a fracture through part of the earth's solid outer zone along which the rock bodies on each side have moved relative to each other.

**Fumarole:** a small vent in a volcanic area through which heated ground water (steam), hydrogen sulphide, or other gases issue.

**Glacier:** a large natural accumulation of ice on land that persists throughout the year and flows downslope under its own weight.

**Granite:** an intrusive igneous rock composed of feldspar, quartz, and minor ferromagnesian minerals.

**Igneous Rocks:** rocks that originate from the cooling and solidification of magma; rocks that cool within the earth's crust are intrusive igneous rocks, and those that cool on the earth's surface are extrusive igneous (volcanic) rocks.

**Lava:** magma that reaches the earth's surface; it cools into extrusive igneous rocks.

**Lava Tube:** a cave or tube up to several feet across formed inside of a lava flow because the interior lava drained away after the top and sides of the flow had cooled and solidified; found mostly in pahoehoe lava.

**Moraine**: landforms composed of till, beneath or at the edges of a glacier; types include ground moraine (beneath a glacier), lateral moraine (ridges along the sides of a valley glacier), and terminal moraine (ridge at the front or terminus of a glacier).

**Polish (glacial)**: smooth, shiny bedrock surface resulting from glacial abrasions; if examined under magnification, polish can be seen to consist of very fine and very closely spaced striations.

**Sediment**: material such as gravel, sand, silt, and clay that has been transported and deposited in layers by an agent of erosion or by precipitation from a solution.

**Shield Volcano**: a large volcano in the shape of an inverted bowl or shield built up almost entirely of numerous lava flows of basalt composition.

**Striation (glacial)**: a scratch or small linear groove cut into a surface of the bedrock by rock fragments carried in a glacier's load; associated with rock surfaces that have experienced glacial abrasion (see polish).

**Talus**: large angular rock fragments that accumulate in an unconsolidated pile at the base of a cliff or steep slope.

**Tarn**: a lake occupying either the floor of a cirque (cirque-tarn) or a bedrock basin in a glaciated valley (trough-tarn).

**Till**: an unconsolidated heterogeneous sediment containing all sizes of fragments from clay to boulders deposited directly by a glacier.

**Volcano**: a more or less conical, circular landform built by the accumulation of lava and/or tephra ejected from a vent; the basic types of volcano include the shield, composite, dome, and tephra cone.

| | AUTHOR'S RATING* | WATER AVAILABLE | WILDLIFE |
|---|---|---|---|
| 1. Brokeoff Mountain | 1 | yes | ● ● |
| 2. Ridge Lakes | 2 | yes | ● ● |
| 3. Sulphur Works | 1 | no | |
| 4. Mill Creek Falls | 2 | yes | ● ● |
| 5. Bumpass Hell continuing to Kings Creek Picnic Area | 1 | yes | ● partl▶ |
| 6. Lassen Peak | 2 | no | |
| 7. Terrace, Shadow, Cliff and Summit Lakes | 2 | yes | |
| 8. Soda Lake | 2 | yes | ● ● |
| 9. Paradise Meadow via Terrace Lake Trail | 1 | yes | |
| 10. Southwest Campground via Cold Boiling and Crumbaug Lakes and Conard Meadows | 1 | yes | ● partl |
| 11. Twin Meadows | 2 | yes | ● ● |

* Rated 1 to 3

1. Suitable for handicapped people

A   Most Difficult
B   Less Difficult
C   Least Difficult

| GEOTHERMAL ACTIVITIES | DEGREE OF DIFFICULTY | SWIMMING | WILDFLOWERS | FOREST | SCENIC VIEWS | TRAILHEAD | GEOLOGICAL FEATURES | TIME | BOATING | FISHING | DISTANCE |
|---|---|---|---|---|---|---|---|---|---|---|---|
| A | | ● | ● | | ● | Park Road Post #2 | ● | 4 hrs. | | | 3.5 miles (5.7 km) |
| A | ● | ● | ● | | ● | Park Road Post #5 | | 1½ to 2 hrs. | | | 1.0 miles (1.6 km) |
| (1) | | | | | | Park Road Post #5 | | 1/2 hr. | | | .2 of a mile (.3 km) |
| C | | ● | ● | | | Park Road S.W. Campground | | 2 to 2½ hrs. | | | 1.6 miles (2.6 km) |
| B | | ● | ● | | ● | Park Road Post #17 | ● | 2½ hrs. | | | 4.0 miles (6.5 km) |
| A | | | | | ● | Park Road Post #22 | | 3 to 4 hrs. | | | 2.5 miles (4.0 km) |
| B | ● | ● | ● | | | Park Road Post #27 | ● | 2½ hrs. one way | | | 3.9 miles (6.3 km) |
| A | | ● | | | ● | Park Road Post #22 | ● | 3½ hrs. | | | 2.0 miles (3.2 km) |
| B | | ● | ● | | | Park Road Post #27 | | 2 to 2½ hrs. | | | 1.6 miles (2.6 km) |
| B | ● | ● | ● | | | Park Road Post #30 | | 3½ to 4 hrs. | | | 5.1 miles (8.2 km) |
| B | | ● | ● | | | Park Road Post #30 | ● | 2½ to 3 hrs. | | | 2.3 miles (3.8 km) |

| | AUTHOR'S RATING* | WATER AVAILABLE | WILDLIFE |
|---|---|---|---|
| 12. Sifford Lakes, return via Bench Lake and Kings Creek Falls | 1 | yes | | |
| 13. Hat Lake to Paradise Meadows | 2 | yes | | |
| 14. Hat Lake to Soap Lake | 3 | yes | • | • |
| 15. Kings Creek Falls | 1 | yes | | |
| 16. Reflection Lake from Manzanita Lake area | 2 | no | • | |
| 17. Manzanita Lake | 2 | no | • | |
| 18. Chaos Crags and Chaos Crags Lake | 2 | yes | | |
| 19. Manzanita Creek | 2 | yes | | |
| 20. Summit Lake to Cluster Lakes, return via Upper Twin and Echo Lake Detour to Badger Flat | 1 | lake | • | • |
| 21. Summit Lake to Lower and Upper Twin via Corral Meadow and Grassy Swale, return via Echo Lake | 1 | yes | • | • |
| 22. Kelly Camp to Corral Meadow to Warner Valley Campground via Flatiron Ridge | 2 | yes | • | • |
| 23. Drakesbad to Kings Creek via Sifford Lakes, return via Kings Creek Falls and Corral Meadow | 1 | yes | • | • |

| GEOTHERMAL ACTIVITIES | DEGREE OF DIFFICULTY | SWIMMING | WILDFLOWERS | FOREST | SCENIC VIEWS | TRAILHEAD | GEOLOGICAL FEATURES | TIME | BOATING | FISHING | DISTANCE |
|---|---|---|---|---|---|---|---|---|---|---|---|
|  | B | • | • | • | • | Park Road Post #32 |  | 3 to 3½ hrs. |  |  | 2.8 miles (4.5 km) |
|  | A | • | • |  |  | Park Road Post #42 |  | 2 to 2½ hrs. |  |  | 1.4 miles (2.2 km) |
| • | A |  |  | • |  | Park Road Post #41 |  | 4½ hrs. one way |  |  | 8.6 miles (13.9 km) |
|  | C | • | • |  |  | Park Road Post #32 |  | 2 hrs. |  |  | 1.2 miles (1.9 km) |
|  | C |  |  | • |  | Park Road Post #65 |  | 1/2 hr. |  |  | .6 of a mile (1.0 km) |
|  | C |  |  | • |  | Park Road Post #66 |  | 1 hr. | • | • | 1.5 miles one way (2.4 km) |
|  | A | • | • | • |  | Manzanita Camp Road |  | 2½ hrs. |  |  | 1.8 miles one way (2.9 km) |
|  | A | • | • |  |  | Manzanita Lake Campground |  | 3½ to 4 hrs. |  |  | 3.5 miles one way (5.7 km) |
| • | A | • | • | • | • | Summit Lake |  | 6 hrs. plus extra time for swimming plus 2 hrs. for Badger Flat |  |  | 10.7 miles (17.3 km) 5.2 miles detour to Badger Flat |
| • | A | • | • | • | • | Summit Lake |  | 6½ hrs. plus additional time for swimming |  | • | 11.1 miles (18.0 km) |
|  | A | • | • |  |  | Kelly Camp |  | 4 hrs. plus fishing time |  | • | 6.3 miles (10.2 km) |
|  | A | • | • |  |  | Warner Valley Campground |  | 6 hrs. |  | • | 11.4 miles (18.5 km) |

| | AUTHOR'S RATING* | WATER AVAILABLE | WILDLIFE | |
|---|---|---|---|---|
| 24. Drakesbad to Dream Lake | 3 | yes | | |
| 25. Drakesbad to Devil's Kitchen via Drake Lake | 1* | yes | | |
| 26. Drakesbad to Terminal Geyser via Boiling Springs and Little Willow Lake | 1 | no | • | • |
| 27. Juniper Lake Ranger Station to Lower Twin Lake via Cameron Meadows and Horseshoe Lake, return via Grassy Swale | 1 | yes | • | • |
| 28. Juniper Lake Campground to Mt. Harkness, return on its west side and south side of Juniper Lake | 1 | no | • | • |
| 29. Juniper Lake Road to Crystal Lake | 1 | lake | | |
| 30. Juniper Lake Ranger Station to Snag Lake, return via Horseshoe Lake | 1 | yes | • | • |
| 31. Ranger Station, Juniper Lake to Butte Lake via Jakey Lake, Red Cinder Cone and Widow Lake | 2 | lake | • | • |
| 32. Juniper Lake Ranger Station to Inspiration Point | 1 | no | | |
| 33. Around Juniper Lake | 3 | no | • | |

* Drake Lake rated at 3
** If Drake Lake eliminated rate as B

| | THERMAL ACTIVITIES | DEGREE OF DIFFICULTY | SWIMMING | WILDFLOWERS | FOREST | SCENIC VIEWS | TRAILHEAD | GEOLOGICAL FEATURES | TIME | BOATING | FISHING | DISTANCE |
|---|---|---|---|---|---|---|---|---|---|---|---|---|
| | ● | | | | | | Parking lot west of Warner Valley Campground | | 1 hr. | | | .7 of a mile one way (1.1 km) |
| ** | ● | | | | ● | ● | Parking lot west of Warner Valley Campground | | 4 to 4½ hours | | | 7.1 miles (11.5 km) |
| | | | | | ● | ● | Parking lot west of Warner Valley Campground | | 3 to 3½ hours | | | 2.7 miles one way (4.3 km)1.1 miles Little Willow Lake |
| | ● | | ● | ● | ● | ● | Juniper Lake Ranger Station | | 7 to 7½ hrs. | ● 1 | ● 1 | 14.0 miles (22.7 km) |
| | | | | | ● | ● | Juniper Lake Campground | ● | 3 to 3½ hrs., 2½ hrs. for direct return | ● 1 | | 5.5 miles (8.9 km) |
| | ● | | | | | ● | .3 of a mile north of Juniper Lake Campground | ● | 1/2 hr. plus time at lake | | ● | .8 of a mile (1.3 km) Round trip |
| | ● | | ● | ● | ● | ● | Juniper Lake Ranger Station | | 4½ hrs. | ● 1 | ● 1 | 6.9 miles (11.2 km) |
| | ● | | ● | ● | ● | | Juniper Lake Ranger Station | ● | 8 hrs. | ● 1,2 | ● 2 | 12.4 miles one way (20.1 km) |
| | | | | | ● | ● | Juniper Lake Ranger Station | ● | 1 hr. | ● 1 | | .6 of a mile (1.0 km) |
| | ● | | | | ● | | Anywhere around the lake | | 3½ to 4 hrs. | ● | | 6.4 miles (10.4 km) |

| | AUTHOR'S RATING* | WATER AVAILABLE | WILDLIFE |
|---|---|---|---|
| 34. Juniper Lake Ranger Station to Warner Valley Road via Horseshoe and Indian Lakes | 1 | lake | ● |
| 35. Butte Lake to Lower Twin via Cinder Cone and Emigrant Trail, return via Rainbow Lake | 2 | lake | ● | ● |
| 36. Butte Lake to Widow Lake and return | 1 | lake | ● | ● |
| 37. Butte Lake to Prospect Peak | 3 | no | | ● |
| 38. Butte Lake Ranger Station to Cinder Cone | 1 | no | | |
| 39. Butte Lake to Bathtub Lake | 2 | no | | |
| 40. Butte Lake to Snag Lake via the east shore of Butte Lake, return via the west shore of Snag Lake | 1 | yes | ● | |
| 41. Pacific Crest Trail | 1 | yes | ● | ● |

1. At Juniper Lake
2. At Butte Lake

| THERMAL ACTIVITIES | DEGREE OF DIFFICULTY | SWIMMING | WILDFLOWERS | FOREST | SCENIC VIEWS | TRAILHEAD | GEOLOGICAL FEATURES | TIME | BOATING | FISHING | DISTANCE |
|---|---|---|---|---|---|---|---|---|---|---|---|
| • | | | | • | • | Juniper Lake Ranger Station | | 3 to 3½ hrs. | •<br>1 | | 6.9 miles (11.2 km) |
| • | | | | • | | Butte Lake Ranger Station | | 6½ hrs. | •<br>2 | •<br>2 | 12.3 miles (19.8 km) |
| • | | • | | • | | Butte Lake Parking Area | • | 4½ hrs. | •<br>2 | •<br>2 | 3.6 miles one way (5.8 km) |
| •<br>2 | | | | • | • | Guide Post 13 of Self Guiding Nature Trail to Cinder Cone | • | 4 hrs. | •<br>2 | •<br>2 | 2.8 miles (4.4 km) |
| •<br>2 | | | | • | • | Butte Lake Ranger Station | • | 2½ to 3 hrs. | •<br>2 | •<br>2 | 1.4 miles (2.2 km) to base of Cinder Cone |
| • | | | | • | • | Butte Lake Parking Lot | • | 45 min. to 1 hr. | •<br>2 | •<br>2 | .4 of a mile (.7 km) |
| • | | • | | • | | Butte Lake Parking Area | | 7 hrs. | •<br>2 | •<br>2 | 12.6 miles (20.4 km) |
| • | | • | | • | • | Little Willow Lake near southern boundary, 4.3 miles east of sign marker #41 near northern boundary | • | 2 days | | | 18.4 miles (29.8 km) |

# Lassen's Pines and Wildflowers

Mountain Hemlock

Ponderosa Pine

Jeffrey Pine

Red Fir

Mariposa Lily

Mountain Mule Ears

False Hellebore

Agoseris

California Stickseed

Water Buttercup

Rabbitbush

Mertens Cassiope

Lupine

Leopard Lily

Newberry Penstemon

Blue Penstemon